Korean Unification and After

The Challenge for U.S. Strategy

Robert Dujarric

HUDSON
INSTITUTE

Korean Unification
and After:
The Challenge for
U.S. Strategy

ISBN 1-55813-070-5

Printed in the United States of America.

For information about obtaining additional copies of this or other Hudson Institute publications, contact:

Hudson Institute
Herman Kahn Center
5395 Emerson Way
Indianapolis, IN 46226, U.S.A.
Fax: 317-545-9639
1-888-554-1325
www.hudson.org

For media and speaking engagement purposes: 317-545-1000 or info@hudson.org

TABLE OF CONTENTS

ACRONYMS

CFC .... Combined Forces Command
DMZ .... Demilitarized Zone (between North and South Korea)
DPRK .... Democratic People's Republic of Korea (North)
ICBM .... Intercontinental Ballistic Missile
IMF .... International Monetary Fund
KMT............... Kuomintang
NATO .... North Atlantic Treaty Organization
PRC .... People's Republic of China
RMA .... Revolution in Military Affairs
ROK............... Republic of Korea (South)
SDF .... Self-Defense Forces (Japanese)
USFJ............... United States Forces, Japan
USFK .... United States Forces, Korea

BIBLIOGRAPHY AND FOOTNOTES

The footnotes provide summary bibliographical data. Full bibliographical references may be found in the bibliography (pages 101–105).

ACKNOWLEDGMENTS

First and foremost, Hudson Institute would like to thank The Korea Foundation for its generous support of this project. This book would not have been possible without the Foundation's help.

The research for this report was made much easier thanks to the assistance of our hard-working interns, Hagiwara Yuko, Joseph King, David Lam, Sarah Peterson, and Martine Price. The work done by Erica Meyer for a previous project also contributed to the research for this book. Hudson Institute Library and Rebecca Cline were also very helpful.

My colleagues at Hudson Institute, Cho Myoung-gyon, Hong Yunsik, and Yoshizaki Tomonori, helped me gain a better understanding of Asian affairs and provided comments on my ideas. Brian Sullivan read parts of the manuscript and made very useful suggestions. Tanaka Yoshiko, who initiated the Washington and Tokyo Korea-Japan Dinner seminars, organized several very helpful sessions in Tokyo, thanks to the hospitality of Dr. and Mrs. Kent Calder, where I was able to discuss my ideas with a group of experts. In Washington, the Korea-Japan Dinner participants have also helped to provide an exciting venue for discussion of Asian security issues. Numerous other individuals in Seoul, Tokyo, and Washington kindly granted me interviews and shared their views with me.

General William E. Odom, whose book *Trial After Triumph* helped me frame my understanding of Asian affairs, provided many useful insights and comments, and suggested the title for this book.

Finally, F. R. Ruskin deserves much of the credit for transforming a manuscript into a publication written in proper English. At Hudson, Christopher Mann and Sam Karnick managed the book publication.

Obviously, I am solely responsible for any errors and omissions that may remain in this book. The views expressed do not necessarily reflect the opinion of The Korea Foundation or Hudson Institute or its sponsors.

Robert Dujarric
Hudson Institute

ABOUT THE AUTHOR

Robert Dujarric is a research fellow in the national securities department at Hudson Institute's Washington, D.C., office. Dujarric, who joined Hudson Institute in 1993, currently researches Northeast Asian security and European affairs.

From 1989 to 1993, he was an associate in the mergers and acquisitions department at Goldman Sachs International Limited in London. Previously, he was an investment banker with the First Boston Corp. in New York and a consultant to the Investment Banking Department at First Boston Limited in New York, Madrid, and Tokyo.

Dujarric holds an MBA from the School of Management at Yale University and a bachelor's degree in government from Harvard University.

PUBLICATIONS

He is coauthor with William E. Odom of *Commonwealth or Empire? Russia, Central Asia, and the Transcaucasus* (Hudson Institute, 1995) and principal author and editor of *Korea: Security Pivot in Northeast Asia* (Hudson Institute, 1998). He coauthored, with Gary L. Geipel, Hudson Executive Briefing *Europe 2005: The Turbulence Ahead and What It Means for the United States* (1995) and four Hudson Briefing Papers: *Russia and the Islamic Threat* (January 1994), *America and Europe: The Risks of Isolationism* (October 1994), *Taiwan and East Asian Security* (February 1996), and *Toward a Coherent U.S. Policy in Northeast Asia* (July 1996). He has also contributed articles to *Strategic Review*, *Commentaire*, Roll Call's *Asia Policy Briefing*, *International Politics and Society*, and the *Los Angeles Times*.

For information about securing Robert Dujarric for your next executive retreat, panel discussion, conference, or executive briefing, contact **Hudson Institute Speakers Bureau** at 317-545-1000. For Mr. Dujarric's latest research on international relations, contact your local bookstore for the current edition of Hudson Institute's quarterly magazine, *American Outlook*, or call 317-545-1000.

PREFACE

This report deals with the issues that will confront the United States after Korean unification or some form of radical transformation in the North puts an end to the North Korean threat. It will also discuss the policies the United States might adopt in a post-unification world.

The danger from North Korea forces the United States to maintain a military presence in South Korea as well as in Japan, which serves as the rear area for the defense of Korea. Because North Korean belligerence is the most obvious justification for America's military deployment in the region, the end of North Korea as we know it could generate a major reappraisal of U.S. defense policy in Asia. This study will address the question of what will happen to American policy in Northeast Asia if the North Korean threat vanishes.

Although Korean unification is now thought to be a remote possibility, the nature of the North Korean state makes it difficult to affirm with any certainty that it can survive the next decade or even the next 12 months. Therefore, policy-makers should be prepared for a sudden collapse. Moreover, even if Korea remains divided and North Korea continues to be a major threat to the Republic of Korea, many of the issues discussed here are relevant to analysts and government officials who deal with Asia policy.

This report concludes that the United States and its allies should plan for a large and prolonged U.S. military presence in Korea and Japan after Korean unification. The study, however, also presents arguments against such a position. Few analysts would agree either with all of the reasoning in favor of a strong presence or with all of the arguments against it, and even strong proponents of one course of action recognize the validity of some of the logic of the other side.

INTRODUCTION

Following the North Korean invasion of the South on June 25, 1950, President Harry Truman decided to defend the Republic of Korea. Almost immediately after the attack, he dispatched U.S. forces to the Korean Peninsula to repel the communist invaders. American soldiers have remained in Korea ever since to deter, and if need be to defeat, another North Korean attack. For half a century, this U.S. military commitment has been a defining element of American policy in Asia. There are several reasons why the transformation of a "police action" against North Korea has become an open-ended stationing of American military personnel (currently 36,000) in a distant Asian nation.

First, over 50,000 Americans died during the Korean War, and the United States put its credibility on the line when it signed the 1953 armistice agreement. To "lose" Korea to the communists would have severely weakened America's containment policy during the Cold War and encouraged further Marxist inroads. Though the Soviet Union is history, American interests, influence, and prestige would still suffer greatly if the United States did not successfully protect the ROK against an attack by the North.

Second, abandoning South Korea to the communists would be seriously detrimental to Japan and Japanese-American relations. In the Soviet era, it would have brought the Soviet bloc closer to Japan.[1] In the post–Cold War environment, a war in Korea, let alone a North Korean victory, would still be a catastrophe for Japan. The conflict could affect Japan through missile strikes, commando raids, flow of refugees, nuclear fallout, and the end of the Korean-Japanese trade and investment relationship. It would also put American reliability into question and thus undermine the American-Japanese alliance.

Third, Korea has gradually become an important U.S. economic partner in its own right and, since the late 1980s, a fellow liberal democracy. Consequently, there is an added economic and ideological dimension to the ROK–U.S. partnership. The election of Kim Dae-Jung, whom the United States saved from execu-

---

1. North Korea was not a full-fledged Soviet satellite, but its reliance on the Soviet Union put it in the Soviet sphere.

tion while he was jailed in Korea and who later sought asylum in the United States, has reinforced the moral bond between the two countries.

Keeping U.S. forces in Korea is largely instrumental in the prevention of war. The North is less likely to attack knowing it would have to fight U.S. forces, and if it did invade, it would be much more difficult for the U.S.–ROK forces to win if the United States did not already have army and air force units in place.

In the Soviet era, Soviet expansionism was another reason for the United States to deploy forces in Asia. But with the breakup of the Soviet Union, North Korea has become the largest tangible military threat to American allies in Northeast Asia. China, although hostile, is not a major military menace to the United States because of geography (bodies of water separate China from Japan and Taiwan, and North Korea is a buffer between China and South Korea) and military weakness. In addition, Beijing's anti–U.S. aims are mitigated by political and economic factors that cause it to avoid war with the United States and its allies. Deterring a Chinese attack against Taiwan requires American forces in Asia—but not as many as are currently deployed, not in the same location, and of a different type. Russia, although unpredictable, is not a danger to U.S. interests in Asia.

Although North Korea is small and very poor, it is a major threat to the ROK, Japan, and the United States. Its location and allocation of resources allow it to remain a significant military power despite its poverty. This totalitarian state has continued to pour resources into its military, to the detriment of other needs, and has benefited from the aid program enshrined in the 1994 Agreed Framework (whereby South Korea, Japan, and the United States pay North Korea in exchange for its pledge to put part of its nuclear bomb manufacturing on hold) and other arrangements. It has also manipulated its food shortage to obtain foreign assistance, which has transferred the burden of feeding segments of the population to foreign governments and charities. The potency of the DPRK's conventional forces may have been degraded by the economic crisis, but it has developed a ballistic missile and weapon of mass destruction program, and its repeated incursions into South Korean territory indicate that it has covert and special operations assets. Moreover, the demarcation of the 1953 armistice line puts

Seoul and other parts of northern South Korea at the mercy of the North's rocket launchers and artillery. Seoul contains 24 percent of the South's population and is the economic and cultural, as well as political, capital of the country. The entire nation would suffer if this metropolis came under attack and there ensued a mass exodus, which itself could be more damaging than an enemy strike. Sharing the same language and ethnicity as the South, the North could also place soldiers dressed in ROK military and police uniforms in the South to create confusion and possible panic during the battle.

The United States successfully deterred Soviet nuclear and missile forces that were many times more potent than those of North Korea. The likelihood of a North Korean nuclear strike against South Korea, Japan, or the United States is thus very low, but the North's capability has created a climate of apprehension in Japan. If North Korea fires missiles equipped with nuclear warheads, casualties could be very high because, for example, the Tokyo-Yokohama metropolitan area is home to more than 11 million people and Osaka has 2.6 million residents. Japan also lacks basic civil defense infrastructure (e.g., most Japanese houses do not even have basements). Therefore, even rockets with poor accuracy can kill large numbers of Japanese if targeted at these cities. Even without the North's use of nuclear weapons, a missile strike could lead, just as in Seoul, to mass hysteria caused by real or imaginary fears of chemical, radioactive, or biological agents. As North Korea proceeds with its ICBM program, it will also have the capability to hit targets in the United States.[2]

South Korea and the United States would prevail against North Korea, but the cost of even a few hours of a North Korean shelling of Seoul, possibly with chemical, biological, or nuclear weapons, would be enormous. Consequently, given North Korea's aggressive behavior and its military posture, it is logical for the United States to maintain military forces in South Korea and Japan to deter North Korea, and almost no one in the United States questions this. However, because North Korean belligerency is the most obvious justification for America's military deployment

---

2. See "North Korea's Coming ICBM," by Larry Niksch, February 10, 1999. http://www.nautilus.org/napsnet/fora/9903A_Niksch.html

in the region, the end of North Korea could start a major review of American defense policy in Asia. This study will address the question of what would happen to U.S. forces in Northeast Asia if the North Korean threat were to vanish.

A winning side's policies after victory can either consolidate its achievements or waste them. It was Tokugawa Ieyasu's skills in forging a durable and peaceful regime of inter-han relations that allowed him to transform his martial successes over his rivals into an effective shogunate that ensured more than two centuries of peace. The allies who defeated Napoleon did not cease their efforts with his abdication, but established a balance of security in Europe that kept the peace for half a century.[3] Thanks to the work of the Congress of Vienna, the energy put forth to defeat the Corsican was rewarded by decades without major wars. After World War I, the allies did not achieve anything more than an armistice for a couple of decades, which owed more to the need of the participants to regenerate their war potential than to the success of the peace treaties. Because of the failures of the 1918–19 settlement, the millions of soldiers who perished during World War I died mostly in vain.

North Korea's demise will not be an event comparable to the end of the Napoleonic Wars or World War I, but the fate of strategically located small states can have far-reaching consequences. East Germany and Yugoslavia, roughly comparable in size and population to North Korea, illustrate this point. Bonn and Washington successfully handled the absorption of the German Democratic Republic (GDR) into the Federal Republic. The cause of peace was strengthened by orchestrating a settlement that was acceptable to all concerned parties without compromising the interests of Germany, the rest of Western Europe, and the United States. In contrast, the incompetence of the United States and the European Union in the face of the fragmentation of Yugoslavia shows how a small country's collapse can affect an entire continent for the worse. Although they enjoyed total military superiority over the various Yugoslav factions, the NATO nations failed to prevent

---

3.　The Congress of Vienna is often credited with a century of peace (1815–1914), but German and Italian unification, Austrian weakness after 1866, French defeat in 1870–71, and colonialism really changed the parameters of the equation and created a new international system in Europe by 1871.

wars and massacres. After years of feckless behavior, the West only imposed a Band-Aid solution in Bosnia that did not stop further conflict in the Balkans and kept war criminals in power in Croatia and Serbia. Thus, a good development—the collapse of a communist dictatorship—turned into a catastrophe for the people of Yugoslavia, fed further conflict in the Balkans, damaged European unity, and humiliated NATO.

It would be wrong, therefore, to assume that unification of Korea would automatically bring peace and stability to Northeast Asia. Well-managed, it could be as successful as Germany's; but improperly handled, it could generate new sources of conflict and instability and rekindle old ones.

1

THE FUTURE
OF KOREA

*T*he end of the North Korean menace is a concept that encompasses several possible developments. The most radical and probable one is the unification of the entire Peninsula under the South Korean regime. Alternatively, North Korea could remain a separate state, but with most of its army demobilized, its missiles and nuclear weapons dismantled under international supervision, and its relations with the South normalized. A middle course would be a confederation or federation, possibly as a transition toward unification. Peaceful coexistence, however, is likely to be only a brief transitional stage toward a unified Korea. The gravitational pull of the South will be hard to resist, and because of the legacy of Kim Il Sung it is nearly impossible that North Korea could become a stable and healthy society on its own. Despite their differences, all these scenarios—unification, confederation, federation, and peaceful coexistence—would alter the strategic environment along the same lines because they would all end the North Korean military threat.

What are the chances of a breakdown of the North Korean regime? Following the collapse of Soviet communism, many thought that North Korea's days were numbered.[4] North Korea

---

4. The paragraphs that follow were first published in *American Outlook*, no. 3, Winter 1999.

has, however, survived. It is nevertheless possible, if not probable, that the DPRK will not last another decade. Communist polities are strong but brittle. They cannot reform because once rulers tinker with them they lose control and the regime collapses.[5] Because a rigid secular catechism underpins the regime, communist parties risk losing their vital ideological underpinnings once capitalist-style changes are introduced. The Gorbachev era was a brief transitional phase that led to the breakdown of the USSR rather than its reformation. *Perestroika*, "Goulash communism" in Hungary, and "Eurocommunism" in Italy, were short, dead-end streets. North Korea's *juche* ideology is somewhat different from European Marxism-Leninism, but its system shares the basic ideological and political characteristics of the Soviet Union, i.e., no private property, single-party government for more than half a century, militarized economy, ideological indoctrination, and very limited and controlled intercourse with the outside world. Consequently, reforms would be unlikely to have a different impact in North Korea than they did in the USSR. This explains why Kim Jong Il, having witnessed the demise of European communism, has avoided any significant change of direction, preferring to let his people starve rather than put his rule at risk.

While the probability of a peaceful market-style reform in Korea is very low, the possibility of a regime breakdown cannot be ignored. A coup could overthrow the Kim Jong Il regime. Alternatively, even the very limited opening to South Korea, coupled with the economic crisis, could undermine social controls. Reports of corruption among North Korean border guards and officials are a sign that the regime may be losing its grip, despite its efforts to maintain the current totalitarian infrastructure. Another possibility is that a failed act of brinkmanship could lead to war with the United States and put an end to the regime.

Regardless of how North Korea collapses, the timing of its breakdown likely will be unexpected. Not many analysts foresaw the demise of the Bourbon and Palavi dynasties, East Germany, the USSR, and Yugoslavia. Moreover, even in cases where some observers were prescient, bureaucratic inertia or the weight of

---

5.   See, for example, William E. Odom, *The Collapse of the Soviet Military*.

conventional wisdom induced governments to ignore them. The seclusion of North Korea makes it difficult to gather data about the country, and even if it were relatively open as were the Soviet Union and Yugoslavia, it is quite possible that foreign officials would fail to understand the information available to them and still be surprised by developments they had not foreseen. Thus, one cannot predict with any certainty that North Korea will be around in 10 years, and much evidence supports the thesis that the regime's years, if not days, are numbered.

Some would argue China shows that reform is possible in communist societies. The Communist Party has, at least until today, escaped collapse through controlled reform, but North Korea's situation is different. First, if liberalization takes place, North Koreans will see that South Koreans are rich and free. This realization will sap not only the legitimacy of the *regime* but also of the *state,* once Northerners realize the extent of the failure of the DPRK to provide for their welfare. Second, North Korea has been communist for 55 years, whereas China had less than 30 years of communist rule when Deng Xiaoping betrayed Maoism. Given the length of communist rule in North Korea, only a few old citizens remember life before Kim Il Sung took over. Thus, the gradual reintroduction of market mechanisms would be harder than it was in China, because there is almost no one in North Korea who has experience with the noncommunist way of life. Third, North Korea is an industrial society (perhaps 60 percent of its citizens are in nonagricultural activities, though many are now idle due to the economic crisis) and is therefore hampered by a large and unproductive industrial sector that would respond less effectively to market reforms than China's huge agricultural workforce (about 75 percent of the population in 1979) when Deng freed the peasantry from full-fledged communism. When farmers are liberated from communist constraints, they can rapidly increase their output and raise their standard of living. If antiquated factories were deregulated, however, they would often be forced to close down or continue to operate at a loss because the price customers would pay for their goods is lower than the marginal cost. Peasants also require few stable institutions; they can sell their grains and buy fertilizer even if there are no clear ownership and commercial laws. Reforming an industrial economy, however, demands a solid legal infrastructure to convince investors to risk their money. (China has partly escaped this predicament because its size mesmerizes investors, who see more than a billion customers, but North Korea does not have this advantage.) Finally, it has yet to be proven that the Chinese experiment with "market socialism" will ensure the survival of the Chinese communists for another decade. It may well turn out, like *perestroika*, to have been the last stage of communist rule.

While we cannot predict if and when North Korea will change, we can say there is a significant probability that by 2010 Korea will either be unified or North Korea will have ceased to be a danger to the South. Because the implications of an end to the North Korean threat are so important, it is desirable that decision makers and analysts focus on this question well before unification becomes a reality. Moreover, most of the issues that will confront the United States after the disappearance of the North Korean threat already face American policy-makers, though in less acute form. Thus, even if North Korea survives in its present form, the United States will have to address many of the potential problems described in this study.

Korea should first be viewed in the context of America's worldwide strategy. Once global issues have been surveyed, this study will identify major Asian security issues and discuss how they will be affected by change on the Korean Peninsula. Finally, this study will look at what kinds of forces the United States might deploy in Asia after the North Korean threat ends.

NORTHEAST ASIA IN U.S. POLICY

Since the end of the Cold War, many Americans have feared the dangers that emanate from non-state sources, such as drug trafficking, transnational crime, and humanitarian crises, or of terrorism, which can be the work of small and weak nations.[6] The collapse of North Korea would allow those who are preoccupied by these "new" threats to challenge the current policy of

---

6.   See opinion poll by the Chicago Council on Foreign Relations, http://
     www.ccfr.org/publications/opinion/opinion.html. See also *The Economist*,
     "Views from the Summit," March 27, 1999, p. 28 (U.S. edition).

allocating a significant fraction of U.S. military might to Northeast Asia.[7]

Many Americans, both among the public at large and the policy-making community, hold the belief that new dangers, different from the traditional threats posed by large military establishments, are becoming a major threat to American security. Secretary of Defense William S. Cohen himself noted the need for "increased attention to terrorism, environmental degradation, emerging infectious diseases, drug trafficking and other transnational challenges" in his introduction to a 1998 report.[8]

These new threats fall into several categories:

- Terrorist attacks by governments of Third World states and nebulous networks of "fanatics";
- Drug trafficking, which feeds crime and addiction in the United States;
- Environmental degradation;
- The breakdown of governments in neighboring countries, making the United States vulnerable to large floods of refugees;
- Humanitarian crises that require external involvement (Rwanda, for example); and
- The spread of new diseases. Although the United States has a low rate of HIV infection (about 0.25 percent), epidemics cannot be contained by borders, and highly contagious diseases, for example, Ebola, could endanger Americans.[9]

This view of international threats has dramatic implications for the defense posture of the United States, particularly for its Asian policy. First, these concerns put a premium on relations between the United States and the Third World, especially the Caribbean littoral (drugs, crime, migration), the Middle East (terrorism), and tropical countries (deforestation, disease), because these countries are the sources of many of these issues.

---

7. This section of this chapter was published in *American Outlook*, Summer 1999 edition.

8. William S. Cohen, *The U.S. Security Strategy for the East-Asia Pacific*, Nov. 1998, p. 1.

9. For more information on Ebola hemorrhagic fever, see http://www.cdc.gov (Centers for Disease Control).

Second, these dangers require the development of worldwide multilateral diplomacy. Achieving results on transnational questions, such as pollution, requires the cooperation of most members of the United Nations and countless nongovernmental organizations (NGOs) that play a role in these discussions.

Third, a focus on these new problems requires a new type of U.S. military. Elite forces for covert action and long-range bombers and missiles for air strikes (which, regardless of their efficacy, give the impression that the government is doing something) are the principal military tools of counter-terrorism, along with intelligence. Fighting illegal drug businesses also calls upon small U.S. units assisting local militaries, U.S. Coast Guard patrols, and the cooperation of the U.S. Navy and Air Force to provide intelligence on the whereabouts of the planes and ships that ferry narcotics. Training the U.S. military for police work, sanitation, repairing utilities, and other civilian tasks is critical for many of the interventions in underdeveloped nations, such as in Haiti, because American soldiers and marines must take over all of the civilian functions that these failed states cannot perform (Ralph Peters, a noted military thinker, calls these interventions "janitorial wars").

Further, as a result of these global threats, domestic programs, such as the Office of National Drug Control Policy, and agencies including the Customs Service; Drug Enforcement Agency; Bureau of Alcohol, Tobacco and Firearms; Border Patrol; National Institutes of Health; Federal Aviation Administration; Secret Service; Immigration and Naturalization Service; Federal Emergency Management Administration; Federal Bureau of Investigation; and local and state police and fire departments, are seen as part of a global policy of securing the United States from these new challenges. These programs and agencies are therefore likely to receive increased funding, to the detriment of the warfighting components of the armed services.

Finally, when addressing these threats, America's ties with its Asian and NATO allies become less important. East Asians and Europeans have little interest in Latin America and the Caribbean. Except for some symbolic British support, the allies do not wish to participate in U.S. attacks on suspected terrorists in the Middle East. In multinational forums, America's allies are not much more important than 150 other states and many NGOs. In the military sphere, fighting the war on drugs overseas and sustaining Third World regimes calls for increased cooperation with the armed forces of the underdeveloped world rather than with Korea, Japan, or NATO.

As long as North Korea remains hostile, these concerns about "new threats" will not influence U.S. defense policy toward Korea very much, because of the consensus about the need to deter North Korea. But once North Korea is gone, if U.S. policy-makers are convinced that the United States must direct its national security policy toward new dangers, there will certainly be a major cutback in U.S. military power deployed in Northeast Asia.

Another analysis of American interests, however, focuses on U.S. alliances with the world's rich liberal democracies—Japan, Korea, Australia (and informally with Taiwan), and with NATO because the United States and these core allies represent approximately 17 percent of the world's population but control about 70 percent of the world's wealth.[10] In addition, their share of the planet's top research and development capacity is probably close to 95 percent. Moreover, the United States and its core allies are internally very stable. The combination of their wealth and their strong internal cohesion makes these allies vastly more powerful than other polities. Most countries outside of this zone are economically underdeveloped and politically fragile. Many of their inhabitants suffer from poverty, violence, and corruption, and their rulers worry about coups, bankruptcy, revolutions, riots, civil wars, and insurrections.

Therefore, as long as the United States keeps its Asian and European alliances and is willing to use its leadership and military power when required, it should be able to deal with any major crisis because its opponents will be, by definition, weak, poor, and unstable. Moreover, the major countries outside of the NATO/Japan-Korea zone—China, India, Iran, Russia, Brazil, and South Africa—are heterogeneous and are very unlikely to be able to create any anti-American league.

According to this more traditional view of security policy, the so-called new threats should be given far less weight than the need

---

10. 1998 GDP estimates from OECD and UNCTAD.

to maintain and strengthen the American alliances in Northeast Asia and Europe. Terrorism, although a nuisance, cannot significantly alter events or endanger U.S. and allied interests. Terrorist movements make headlines but do not win wars, and successful guerrillas generally owe their success to a powerful patron (for example, the Vietnamese communists or the Afghan mudjadeens) or to a weak and demoralized adversary (such as the colonial powers after World War II). They are far less dangerous than powerful nations with strong military establishments. Moreover, stable polities like the United States are far less vulnerable to terrorism than most other societies, because terrorist attacks, even if tactically successful, do not threaten the legitimacy of the state. Drug trafficking is financed by domestic American demand (many Americans use drugs and have the money to buy them—and as generally happens, demand generates supply). There is little that military action in the jungles of Colombia can achieve, except to switch the production of drugs from Latin America to labs and farms inside the United States. This would only facilitate the work of the illicit drug industry; American narcotics producers working within the United States enjoy all the constitutional protections of due process that make arrest and conviction more difficult than in Third World nations, and the lines of communication between producer and consumer would be shortened. Refugee migration, rather than being a threat, has actually often benefited the United States—for example, in Florida where Castro's loss became America's gain when Cuban exiles brought their skills and dynamism to Florida. Environmental issues and public health can be important, but they are not national security issues.

The operational implication of this "traditional" view is that the United States should keep strong forces in Korea and Japan for the foreseeable future. Northeast Asia, along with Europe and North America, is one of the three centers of wealth and power in the world. The United States needs to keep a strong defense relationship with the region because any weakening of these transpacific ties could decouple the United States from Northeast Asia. Shorn of alliances with Japan and Korea, the United States would lose the benefits of an alliance with two members of the core group of rich liberal democracies.

U.S. RESOURCES AVAILABLE
FOR NATIONAL DEFENSE

An important question for the United States is whether it has the wherewithal to continue playing a major military role in the region or if the end of the North Korean menace should be a welcome opportunity to jettison an expensive foreign commitment. Many of those who are reluctant to see the United States continue to maintain strong forces in Asia and to remain the regional hegemon in Northeast Asia subscribe to a declinist vision of American power, not dissimilar to the one that justified Richard Nixon's détente policy. Paul Kennedy's *The Rise and Fall of the Great Powers*[11] is seldom quoted now, but his underlying thesis of imperial overstretch is implicitly accepted by many policy analysts.

Because other countries have grown in economic and military might, declinists note that the relative power of the United States has waned considerably in the past 50 years since the zenith of the immediate post–World War II years. Moreover, some proponents of this theory of American decline are concerned by internal problems, which they believe require Americans to focus more on domestic affairs. They point to the underclass, the mediocrity of American primary and secondary schools, the appalling frequency of homicides, and the ever-growing prison population as proof of the fragility of American prosperity.

In this view, the United States must accept its decline and adjust its policies accordingly. Northeast Asia should wean itself from American hegemony and rely on a traditional balance of power between China, Japan, Russia, Korea, Taiwan, and the United States. ("Ultimately, the balance of power in Asia will have to be worked out among Asians."[12]) The United States should also rely more on multilateral institutions to transfer some of the burden of empire onto other shoulders.[13]

---

11. Paul Kennedy, *The Rise and Fall of the Great Powers*.

12. Ronald Steel, "The Hard Questions: Re-Orient." *The New Republic*, Sept. 8 & 15, 1997, p. 27.

13. Douglas T. Stuart and William T. Tow, *A U.S. Strategy for the Asia-Pacific*, is a good example of such thinking.

The traditional declinist school believes that America's relative weight in world affairs has diminished as other nations have become richer and stronger in the past 50 years. There is also a group of American social conservatives who focus on moral, rather than material, decline. They believe that the United States should direct its energy to moral rearmament. Though their concerns are not with international issues, their views have implications for America's international position. First, their focus on domestic issues makes them less interested in America's military posture. This is an important point because, during the Cold War, American conservatives were one of the domestic groups most favorable to an activist foreign policy backed by military power. Second, some conservatives have become increasingly hostile to all things foreign for a variety of ideological and philosophical reasons,[14] making them unable to accept the compromises that are necessary to maintain the alliances required for American hegemony.

Another interpretation of America's position in the world, however, argues not only that the United States is not in decline but also that events in the past 10 years, namely the collapse of the Soviet Union and the demise of communist ideology, have made the United States incomparably more powerful. Moreover, the states whose citizens and corporations own most of the world's wealth outside the United States are the Asian allies of the United States and the NATO nations. The post–World War II recovery of Europe and Japan has lowered the U.S. share of world GDP; but this has relieved the United States of the burden of having to care for its allies, and instead has provided Washington with partners who contribute to the common defense. In 1947, when President Truman enunciated the doctrine that bears his name, the United States was the only large rich country in the world and American taxpayers had to feed most of their allies and former foes. The great tasks of the early Cold War—the reconstruction of Europe, the Ber-

---

14. See Irving Kristol, "The Coming Clash of Welfare States," *American Outlook*, Winter 1999, pp. 57–59.

lin airlift, the Korean War—were underwritten almost exclusively by Americans. In the 1990s, however, Europeans and Japanese have paid tens of billions of dollars for the Gulf War, assistance to former communist states, support for Bosnia's economy, the Bosnian NATO force (I/SFOR), the war in Kosovo in 1999, refugee assistance in Europe, and the defense of Korea and Japan; in addition, European troops have provided the majority of manpower in I/SFOR, the NATO occupation army in Kosovo (KFOR) contributed hundreds of aircraft to the Kosovo War, and both Korea and Japan have modern militaries paid for by their taxpayers.

The United States is also economically stronger now than it was several decades ago. American companies lead the world in most of the key industries of the era—computers, entertainment, software, finance. Moreover, unlike other rich countries of Europe and Asia, the United States is not in demographic decline and has been far more successful at absorbing immigrants. While this situation will not last forever, America will continue to be the world's only superpower for at least several decades if it so desires.

Consequently, for those who perceive the United States as a powerful nation whose strength is increasing, America is more than capable of remaining a world leader. U.S. power is not limitless, but it is more than sufficient to maintain military hegemony in Northeast Asia (and Europe), and the United States should seek to take advantage of the collapse of North Korea to include all of Korea in its sphere. The declinists, however, are unlikely to support a continued American military presence in Asia after Korean unification. They will see the end of the North Korean threat as an opportunity to cut the costs and risks of having forces in Korea and Japan.

STRATEGIC ISSUES FACING THE UNITED STATES

The preceding discussion dealt with the global context of America's defense policy. This section analyzes the issues that the United States will confront in Asia as Korean unification approaches, looking at them from the angle of Korean domestic and foreign policy, U.S.–Japan relations, Korea-Japan relations, Sino-Japanese relations, Sino-Korean relations, Chinese policy, Taiwan, and Russia.

Following Korean unification, or reconciliation, the United States will need to make choices about its role in Asia. The key decisions will be in the military sphere. There might be a need for economic assistance, but U.S. policy regarding trade and investment will not be radically affected; these issues revolve around the economic relationship between the United States and its capitalist economic partners in Asia, first and foremost Japan, rather than with North Korea. Moreover, America's military role is far more important in Asia than its economic role. The United States is the world's largest economy, but Japan and the EU (whose GDP is larger than America's) are also major economic actors and Asia's economy depends primarily on the performance of the Asian economies themselves. In the political realm, however, no country comes close to the United States in military power. Moreover, for historical reasons, the largest American ally in Asia, Japan, faces political, institutional, constitutional, psychological, and diplomatic impediments to the use of its armed forces as a foreign policy tool, further increasing the weight of American military power in Asia.

KOREA AND UNIFICATION

End of the North Korean Menace and Subsequent Unification

The process by which the North Korean regime is eliminated will affect the scale and timing of the challenges that will confront the Republic of Korea. Unification resulting from the defeat of a North Korean armed thrust into the South would be different from a gradual process of reconciliation leading to a Korean confederation. Nevertheless, while the magnitude and time frame of the issues will depend on how unification is achieved, the challenges will remain the same.

Integrating North Korea into the ROK

Since it is unlikely that a reformed North Korean state could survive long before being absorbed by the ROK, it is important to analyze the implications of unification for the ROK. South Korea does not have the expansive and expensive welfare state of West Germany. Therefore, North Korea will not be burdened with the high labor costs and social contributions that discourage employment in eastern Germany by pricing out part of the labor force.[15] Moreover, because North Korea is relatively small, the investment in infrastructure that will be required will be manageable with the help of the international community. North Koreans, unlike East Germans who knew about western wealth, may also have low expectations. They may be satisfied by modest improvements in their lifestyle, such as a better diet and basic health care (though they might quickly want more as they realize how well South Koreans live). In addition, North Koreans should provide a low-cost labor force that South Korean companies could use to produce labor-intensive goods that might otherwise be manufactured in poor Asian nations such as Vietnam or Indonesia.

Nevertheless, the economics of unification will not be easy. Famine or malnutrition may have stunted—physically and intellectually—some children and has surely weakened many Northerners. This will slow economic development because some of the population may suffer from temporary or permanent physical and mental handicaps. In addition, as noted earlier, North Korea is an industrial economy (though much of its production capacity is unused). If most North Koreans were peasants, basic market-ori-

---

15. See article by Han Taejon, "The Cost of Korean Unification and the Role of Foreign Investment," in *Korea and Japan: Toward a New Partnership?* (Robert Dujarric, ed., Hudson Institute, forthcoming).

ented reforms could quickly raise their output and standard of living. Unfortunately, most of North Korea's industrial assets are probably worthless, incapable of producing goods that could be sold for profit. One of its few export earners, the sale of missiles and other weapons to the Middle East and Pakistan, is likely to be halted. Therefore, the North will need to attract investors to build new plants. In addition, substantial effort will be needed to train laborers, used to communist industrial organization, to function in capitalist enterprises. The mining sector, which might provide some jobs after the infrastructure has been rehabilitated, is capital-intensive rather than labor-intensive and will require bringing managers from the South. Before investors arrive, most of the factory workers, as well as idle soldiers (North Korea's army has an estimated 923,000 men,[16] more than the U.S. Army) are likely to be unemployed, and feeding them will be a burden for the national treasury.

Apart from the economic challenge, integrating the people of North Korea into a unified Korean polity will be an arduous task. Almost all North Koreans have known only a regime that has deprived them of all freedoms and denied them access to the outside world. No nation has ever experienced such an extreme and long-lasting form of totalitarianism (Cambodia's was worse, but much shorter; the Soviet Union lasted longer, but except for the Lenin-Stalin era, which persisted less than four decades, it was softer). Free competition in politics, production, and the realm of ideas is totally alien to North Koreans, who are accustomed to the intellectual monopoly of the *juche* idea, the Kim cult, and a command economy. Contact with South Korean society will be a psychological shock for Northerners. They will confront fellow citizens with totally different mentalities, lifestyles, working and leisure habits, and diets. North Koreans will also have to deal with their own ignorance of the Chinese ideographs that are still widely used in South Korean academic work (though in the ROK, too, more and more publications use the Korean phonetic script, *hangul*, in lieu of ideographs). They will also have to learn new words

16. International Institute for Strategic Studies, *The Military Balance 1997/98*, p. 183.

(often derived from English), which are used in the South but not in the North.

Korea has a strong tradition of regionalism, and South Koreans could fear the creation of a large new voting bloc (about one-third of the electorate) in the North, consisting of people who know nothing about democratic politics. The Korean Workers' Party (KWP, the ruling party), even if outlawed, may regroup under a different name[17] and manipulate the newly enfranchised voters. The problem of integrating former communist subjects into the citizenry of a free nation is a complex issue. It was mitigated in Germany by several factors. First, East Germany's autocrats did not impose the same level of totalitarianism as Kim Il Sung and his son did. East Germans drove private automobiles and traveled to other eastern European countries, churches remained open, foreigners walked freely throughout the capital city, and the police tolerated mild forms of dissent. Second, East Germans, thanks to West German TV and radio, and visits from western relatives, were better prepared for life in a liberal democracy. Third, in 1990 East Germans were 21 percent of the German population, versus about 35 percent for northern Koreans in the Peninsula's total population (perhaps a little less if more North Koreans perish because of dire economic circumstances). Fourth, West German liberalism and democracy had stronger roots than South Korea's. Nevertheless, the integration of the eastern Germans has not been smooth. In eastern Germany, the Communist Party, renamed the Party of Democratic Socialism (PDS), managed to obtain 20 percent of the vote in the former GDR in 1998, including 23.6 percent in one state (up from 10 percent in 1990 and 18 percent in 1994).[18] Though the country has been unified for almost a decade, there is still a wide chasm between the two sides, as demonstrated during the Kosovo War of 1999, which westerners supported and easterners opposed. In fact, despite the awesome improvement in the standard of living of eastern Germans since unification, made

17. See Nack Young An, "Korea in the East Asian Dynamic," in *Korea and World Affairs*, Spring 1995.

18. Source: German Federal Statistics Office at http://www.statistik-bund.de. Percentages are for the second (proportional) vote and exclude Berlin.

possible by West German transfer payments, the former communists have managed to increase their electoral scores during the first decade of German unification. The difficulties encountered by all post-communist societies, especially polities like North Korea, which do not have a native noncommunist elite, indicate how hard the road away from communism is. So far, only a few central European countries have made a relatively successful exit from Marxist-Leninist totalitarianism, and none of these nations had endured what North Koreans have been subjected to.

Korean unification is not only analogous to that of Germany in 1990, it also bears some resemblance to the reunification of the United States after the Civil War, because South and North Koreans fought one another in a bloody war where many atrocities occurred (and to this day North Korean soldiers sometimes kill South Korean civilians during operations in the South), unlike East and West Germans who never exchanged fire. Korean communism has also acquired many unique national characteristics (the *juche* idea and the worship of the Kim family), and it may be very difficult to disentangle Northern identity from communism in the minds of both Northerners and Southerners. It is thus possible that the antipathy between both sides will be much stronger than was the case in Germany (and even in eastern Germany many complain of the negative attitudes of western Germans toward their fellow citizens from the east). Richard Grinker's thesis[19] that South Koreans will view unification as a victory against the North and treat Northerners as defeated foes, rather than seeing it as the integration of the long-suffering Northerners into the ROK, suggests that the unification process will be far more difficult than it was in Germany. Even those who do not accept Grinker's conclusions admit that unifying Korea will be internally difficult.

One post-unification alternative for Korea would be to put the North through a period of "guided democracy" in which Southerners would train their new compatriots in the art of living in a free nation. Treating the North like a protectorate in need of re-education, however, could create resentment in North Korea. The western allies imposed this system on West Germany after 1945,

---

19.   Roy Richard Grinker, *Korea and Its Future: Unification and the Unfinished War.*

but they were exercising the traditional rights of invaders to rule over the vanquished. It would be much more difficult for South Korea to do the same, because it would be awkward to "occupy" a part of Korea that had just been liberated. The option, however, of making the North into just another region of the ROK and, for example, having Peninsula-wide elections just after unification, would be unrealistic because the northern voters will lack the socialization necessary for informed voting. Besides casting ballots, there are many aspects of life in a capitalist democracy for which the Northerners are not equipped, and there will thus have to be some form of transitional regime.

The demise of North Korea will also open the door to complex legal and moral issues. Should the leaders of the ruling party be prosecuted for their crimes? How should torturers, camp guards, and other lesser criminals be punished? Should some, or all, members of the party be banned from politics? As events in former communist Europe have shown, there are no easy solutions. Being too soft on the officials of the old regime could run the risk of legitimizing past atrocities and allowing the communists to regroup. Being too harsh could lead to a feeling of victimization in the North, and if Northern leaders fear retribution they could decide to fight to the death. Moreover, in a state like North Korea all the best trained and educated people are, by definition, party members in good standing, and these are the locals best qualified to staff administrative positions, and Koreans may be moved north to provide some managerial talent, but most administrative tasks will have to be performed by locals.

The issue of property rights will also have to be addressed. Many Northerners fled to the South after the communist takeover. They, and their offspring, could claim their ancestral land after the fall of communism. On the one hand, to acquiesce to their desires would displease the Northerners who stayed and would slow economic development while competing claims from people seeking the same real estate or from disagreement among heirs are disentangled. On the other hand, refusal to return their property would create another group of malcontents after unification. The alternative of creating a compensation fund that would indemnify former landlords with cash would add to the financial cost of unification.

The ROK has completed a remarkably effective transition from autocracy to liberal democracy. Kim Young Sam was the first president to complete a full term of office and remain a free man afterward. Former presidents Chun Doo Wan and Rho Tae Woo were tried in court rather than summarily jailed, exiled, or liquidated by their rivals. The Korean press is free, and there are no restrictions on travel abroad. The economy has been significantly liberalized since the days of Park Chung Hee, and the private sector enjoys more freedom than in the 1970s. President Kim Dae Jung's victory and his ability to assume power easily indicate that Korean democracy is stronger than many thought. Nevertheless, liberal democracy is a recent phenomenon in Korea. Political parties are made and unmade because they are often the instrument of individual ambition rather than institutions that can outlive their leaders. The various rumors regarding the anti–Kim Dae Jung activities of the intelligence services during the last presidential elections are another example of the unfinished nature of the democratic transition (they were accused of plotting with North Korea to discredit Kim Dae Jung's candidacy). The economic crisis, which has not yet been fully resolved, could increasingly strain the middle class.

Moreover, the regionalism of Korean politics will also potentially be destabilizing after unification. Regional affiliation, more than ideology, accounts for Korean voting patterns (Kim Dae Jung obtained 92 percent of the vote in his native province of South Cholla in 1992 [and 97 percent in his hometown of Kwangju], whereas Kim Young Sam got 72 percent of the electorate in the South Kyongsang province to support him; by comparison, Bob Dole got 54 percent of the Kansas vote and Bill Clinton 53 percent in Arkansas). Korean regionalism, though not occurring along ethnic, linguistic, or religious lines, reflects a potential for debilitating factionalism, which unification could make even more dangerous if the north of the country became a large alienated province. As a result of these factors, the trauma of unification could undermine Korea's political liberalization and put it, if only temporarily, on a reverse course toward authoritarianism or instability.

The internal problems Korea will face after unification will affect the United States. First, if unification resulted in a period of instability, and possibly even violence, the Peninsula could be at risk, given the large number of soldiers in both Koreas. The United States would have to be concerned for the security of its forces and of American civilians, and mindful of the whereabouts of the North Korean weapons of mass destruction. Much more dangerous than nuclear or chemical arms, which are difficult to use and hard to hide, would be the proliferation of small arms (rifles, pistols, grenades, light machine guns) if a breakdown of order made it possible for demobilized soldiers to keep or sell their weapons or for civilians to steal from depots as happened in Albania. Japan, America's most powerful Asian ally, would also be concerned, and the United States would have to find ways not only to deal with the Korean situation but also to reassure Japan.

Second, if Korea is weakened by the unification process, it will be more difficult for the United States to negotiate agreements on the nature of the post-unification U.S.–Korea relationship. A weak and unstable ROK government, which might face powerful, and possibly violent, opponents, would find it hard to agree on a coherent foreign policy. Americans may also be more reluctant to continue an alliance with Korea if there are doubts about its stability and democracy.

Third, it would be difficult to get Japan's government involved in a closer relationship with Korea if the country is unstable. Moreover, the government in Seoul may not feel sufficiently confident to deal with Japan because latent anti-Japanese feeling in Korea means that a government needs to be strong and self-confident to make overtures to Tokyo. Some xenophobic or protectionist politicians may take advantage of the post-unification turmoil, to the detriment of relations with Japan and the United States.

Moreover, if Korea's liberal democratic order suffers a severe setback following unification, it would further complicate American-Korean cooperation. Ideology is a key component of American policy, and it is easier for the United States to have good relations with free nations than with dictatorial ones—especially those that used to be democracies. Except for Saudi Arabia, whose cultural isolation and oil wealth make it exceptional, all the important allies or partners of the United States are either liberal democracies or states like Turkey and Mexico that have attempted to make some progress in past decades toward that goal.

Other analysts are more optimistic about the future. Korea has now had three peaceful open presidential elections, and Kim Dae Jung, a former death row inmate and archenemy of the establishment, has had little difficulty in establishing his authority over the country. Despite a severe recession, the country has remained democratic and stable. It has avoided the paranoid xenophobia that has infected the Malaysian government. This is a particularly remarkable achievement. Koreans have a strong sense of nationalism and an understandable feeling that they have been subjected to unjust suffering for most of the twentieth century. The country for a long time had a mercantilist-protectionist state ideology opposed to imports and foreign investment. The U.S./IMF–imposed reforms have forced a drastic liberalization in foreign economic relations, while the standard of living has fallen. Despite these factors, however, there has been no "blame the foreigners" campaign on the part of the government, the opposition, or the media.

Thus, for the optimists, unification may strain Korean society, but there is no reason to believe that the ROK will not handle the absorption of the North successfully. The experience of the North Koreans will help Seoul manage the integration of the Northerners because a half-century of tyranny and misery has made them docile. The citizens of the former DPRK will be so thankful for the increase in their standard of living (which will be easy to achieve, given the low starting point) that the government will be able to control the timetable of their gradual political and economic integration without fearing any upheaval.

America's Role in Korean Domestic Affairs

Some would argue that America can contribute to stability during and after unification by keeping its soldiers in Korea. By providing a sense of continuity and support, American forces will lessen the risks to Korea's liberal development. The U.S. military presence will be proof to Koreans and foreigners alike that the United States stands by a democratic Republic of Korea. In case of an emergency, such as civil disturbances in the North, the USFK could assist the ROK armed forces by providing airlift, intelligence, and other support functions short of combat (unless there were a major communist insurrection, the governments of the United States and the ROK would want American soldiers to stay out of inter-Korean fighting).

Others would argue that there will be no need for an American "handholding" operation. The ROK has been democratic for many years now, and, in spite of a few coups, stable since Park Chung-Hee took over in 1961. The murder of President Park and the unrest of the 1980s were ripples on the surface of a society that was peacefully and rapidly achieving middle-class prosperity. Few nations have undergone such rapid urbanization and industrialization as South Korea without major social upheaval. Prior to full democratization, the army hierarchy and technocrats ran the country effectively and fairly. Since the election of Rho TaeWoo, the electoral process has functioned well. Taiwan, Northeast Asia's other recent convert to liberal democracy, has gone through a fine democratic transition without American soldiers stationed on the island, as have Central European nations, whereas U.S. bases did little good for Filipinos. Therefore, Korea, according to this analysis of Korean politics, does not need U.S. forces for its domestic stability.

Another line of thought sees American soldiers as counterproductive because they inflame anti-Americanism. To maintain a good relationship with Korea, Washington should thus remove its forces after the end of the North Korean threat. Unification will be a national victory, and Koreans will not want foreign troops to remain for long in their homeland. Koreans, unlike Europeans, have had little intercourse with foreigners during most of their history. Foreign forces on Korean soil, especially those from a totally alien culture, are abnormal. A continued U.S. presence might also entangle Americans in factional disputes in Korea and damage the U.S.–Korean relationship. Even today, despite the obvious Northern threat, many South Koreans dislike the presence of American soldiers, whom they suspect of sometimes engaging in criminal behavior such as rape and murder. One may also note that the Taiwanese, who have not hosted American forces for a quarter of a century (and even when there were American servicemen in Taiwan they were not as numerous as they are today in Korea), are far less prone to anti-American sentiment than South Koreans.

THE FOREIGN POLICY OF A UNITED KOREA

As long as North Korea threatens the South, the ROK has no viable replacement for the U.S. alliance. The USFK reduces the likelihood of war and the cost of defending the Republic, and there is no credible alternative partner for South Korea. Therefore, it is only after the North Korean problem is solved that Seoul will be able to redefine its foreign policy.

One possibility is that Korean nationalism might reassert itself against the United States. Since Korea was freed from Japan in 1945, the ROK's military dependence on the United States has limited its sovereignty. A U.S. Army general sits at the top of the military chain of operational command of the South Korean armed forces in wartime, and his status must seem proconsular to Koreans. Moreover, some Korean conscripts serve as "Korean Augmentation Troops to the U.S. Army" (KATUSAs) in American military units. When inter-Korean meetings are held in the truce village of Panmunjom, there are American soldiers in the detachment that patrols the southern side of the Joint Security Area. The large compound occupied by the U.S. military in the center of downtown Seoul is a symbol of America's weight in Korean affairs (the American enclave is a large estate with a golf course and U.S.–style houses in the middle of a crowded metropolis where space is at a premium). The fact that the United States defends the ROK does not mitigate the psychological scars caused by America's role in Korea. One need only imagine how Americans would feel if, to save them from Canadian aggression, Korea had 500,000[20] soldiers and airmen in the United States. The Korean general, headquartered on the Washington Mall would exercise operational control over all American military units in case of conflict. Some Korean servicemen, paid far better than American soldiers, would return home with American brides. Korean would be the most popular foreign language in America, and kimchi stalls and theaters showing the latest movies from Seoul would proliferate from coast to coast. Americans would be thankful for protection against the Canadians, but they would also harbor mixed feelings

---

20. Based on the ratio of population between the ROK and the United States the equivalent would be around 230,000 troops, but South Korea is far smaller than the United States, so the visibility of 37,000 Americans in the ROK is far greater than that of 230,000 Koreans would be in the United States.

about Koreans. Yet the culture shock the Americans would experience pales in comparison to that which Koreans have experienced, because the United States is a multiethnic society and 500,000 or even a million additional Korean men would not stand out as much in America as 37,000 mostly white or black English-speakers do in Korea.

Koreans have further reasons to be ambivalent about America. Washington acquiesced to Japan's conquest of Korea in exchange for Japan's consent to the occupation of the Philippines, and Americans ignored Korean suffering (in contrast to U.S. concern for the fate of the Chinese). American bureaucrats cut Korea in half in 1945 without consulting Koreans about it, and U.S. forces made no great effort to apprehend Japanese guilty of war crimes against Koreans. Moreover, because Koreans could not free themselves from Japanese occupation, the United States unwittingly wounded Korean pride by defeating Japan while Koreans stood on the sidelines. In 1953, the United States unilaterally signed an armistice that prolonged the division of Korea despite the opposition of President Rhee. In addition, American cultural influence has not necessarily pleased all Koreans, who may not think that American mores, films, and fast food are what young Koreans need. Others blame the United States for the Kwangju massacres, when ROK Army troops killed civilians in that city.[21] The forced liberalization of Korea's trade and investment regime, spearheaded by the United States, is also distasteful to some Koreans, especially those who fear that their jobs and livelihoods are endangered by American imports and investors.

Consequently, Koreans may take advantage of the end of the threat from the North to remove U.S. forces from Korea and achieve equidistance from the various powers in Asia. Korea may also distance itself from the United States to avoid being drawn into America's perceived anti-Chinese policies. This does not necessarily mean that Korea would follow an anti-American policy,

---

21. Some Koreans thought that the U.S. military was in control of the ROK military and could have prevented them from entering Kwangju. In fact, the United States was not exercising operational control over the ROK units involved, but many Koreans still blamed the United States, which they think is "in command" of ROK troops.

but rather that it would seek to escape the sometimes suffocating embrace of the United States.

Though nationalism may work in favor of minimizing U.S.–Korean security ties, Seoul might nevertheless decide to continue its defense relationship with the United States.[22] The Korean government may conclude that the United States is necessary to provide an "insurance policy" against Chinese "hegemonism" or Japanese "militarism."[23] Russia is weak but could still cause trouble, either by offering opportunities for Chinese expansionism or because of the destabilizing impact of a sick neighbor with a large—albeit disorganized—military. The United States, because of its distance, may thus be the best—or least bad—ally for the country in its quest for security,[24] a conclusion King Kojong already reached in 1883 when he asked for U.S. military advisors because Seoul saw the United States as the only player without colonial ambitions against Korea.[25] The United States is the most powerful nation on the planet, and as a medium-size power, Korea may consider that having an ally that is powerful but far away is the best solution.

Obviously, if Korea decides to sever its alliance with the United States, Washington will have to accept this decision. But, for proponents of a continued U.S. presence, this would be unfortunate. Keeping U.S. soldiers in Korea after unification would strengthen the cause of those who want Korea to remain aligned with the United States, because it would demonstrate U.S. resolve to continue to defend Korea, whereas without American troops in their country, Koreans might have doubts about the U.S. commitment and seek to pursue alternative foreign policies. But at the

---

22. Han Yong-sup, "Korea's Security Strategy for the 21st Century: Cooperation and Conflict," *Korea Focus* 5, no. 4 (July-Aug. 1997), pp. 63–78.

23. Ahn Byong-Joon, "Korea–U.S. Alliance Toward Unification," *Korea Focus* 4, no. 2 (March-April 1996), pp. 5–19. And see "U.S. Forces in a Unified Korea," *Korea Focus* 5, no. 3 (May-June 1997), pp. 143–45.

24. See Kim Sung-Han, "The Future of the Korea–U.S. Alliance," *Korea and World Affairs* 20, no. 2 (summer 1996), pp. 184–196.

25. Lee Dong-Bok, "Remembering and Forgetting: The Political Culture of Memory in Divided Korea," *Korea and World Affairs* (fall 1995), pp. 439–40.

same time, the United States will have to address the possibility that Korean resentment of the United States could create problems, and will need to devise mechanisms to deal with these issues.

U.S.–JAPAN RELATIONS AND KOREAN UNIFICATION

Korean unification will have a major impact on Japan and U.S.–Japan relations. The danger posed by North Korea is one of the justifications for the U.S. presence in Japan. American forces in Japan deter North Korean strikes on Japan because they demonstrate the reality of the U.S.–Japan alliance, making it less likely for North Korea to think that it could hit Japan without U.S. retaliation. The U.S. presence also strengthens Japan's security because Japan contributes to the U.S. military's ability to fight North Korea by providing rear-area bases for U.S. forces in Korea and giving strategic depth to the U.S. arrangements for the defense of Korea. Therefore, as long as North Korea is a danger, the United States is most unlikely to significantly alter its military deployment in Japan.

Once North Korea is removed from the scene, however, the need for U.S. protection may be less obvious. Former Prime Minister Hosokawa Morihiro, in a 1998 *Foreign Affairs* article, called for removing the U.S. military presence from the country by the end of the century.[26] There has always been an opposition movement to the American bases, though its strength has declined since the 1960 riots. But views such as Hosokawa's could gain a greater audience after the demise of North Korea.

Even with the North Korean menace, the American presence in Japan is a delicate issue. Almost all U.S. ground forces in Japan are the marines on Okinawa. Though Okinawa represents only 0.6 percent of Japan's territory, 75 percent of the land used by American forces in Japan and all their ground combat elements are located on that island. Along with memories of the horrible

---

26. Hosokawa Morihiro, "Are U.S. Troops in Japan Needed? Reforming the Alliance," *Foreign Affairs* 77, no. 4 (July-Aug. 1998), p. 5. It is unclear if he meant A.D. 2001 or A.D. 2000 (the next century will actually start on January 1, 2001, not 2000).

battle there in 1945 and the massive destruction suffered during the American invasion, Okinawans must bear social and environmental costs—for example, the use of scarce land for the bases, noise, pollution, and the need to accommodate thousands of single young males, as a result of hosting 16,600 marines and some air force personnel.

The U.S.–Japan Security Treaty and the presence of American troops have had a dramatically positive effect on Japan and the United States. For the first time since the Western invasions of East Asia in the 19th century, Japan's government does not feel that national survival requires imperialist and colonialist expansion. Korea's predicament was its weakness in the face of Japanese, Chinese, Czarist, Bolshevik, and U.S. imperialism. Japan's combativeness resulted from the combination of (a) insecurity caused by the predatory Western powers, and (b) the capabilities of Japan's military might. The post–World War II environment has ended the lethal cycle of insecurity and expansion.

The U.S.–Japan alliance and the U.S. forward deployment in Asia made it possible for Japan to renounce war (Article 9 of the constitution) and to refute the Clausewitzian notion that war is the continuation of policy by other means (because the United States took that task upon itself). By allowing Japan to keep a low military profile, the alliance made it easier for Koreans and other Asians to accept the rise of Japan as Asia's preeminent economy, because Japan could no longer be perceived as a military threat. This is particularly important because Japan's immense economy compared with that of its neighbors could easily make Japan look frightening to other Asians. The failure of Japanese governments to deal effectively with the legacy of the war crimes in Asia in the 1930s and 1940s has severely compounded this problem by damaging Japan's image, and recent Japanese efforts to reverse this error will take many years to yield fruit.

On the Japanese side, there are those who are wary of Korea and suspect it of revanchist goals. The U.S. presence in Asia has not erased this latent hostility and fear. What the United States has achieved is to make it manageable. American military superiority has meant that Koreans and Japanese each knew that the other posed no military threat because the United States was far more powerful than either country and would not tolerate a South Ko-rean–Japanese conflict. Thus the United States has been defend-ing South Korea against Japan and Japan against South Korea. This may surprise Americans, but worries about Japanese "milita-rism" remain a feature of Korean life.

Korean unification will increase the potential for mutual suspicion between Japan and Korea. Seoul and Tokyo will have fewer reasons to cooperate militarily, because of the absence of a mutual (North Korean) enemy. Moreover, Japanese officials know that even if South Koreans worry about Japan, they must devote most of their military effort to deterring the North, a situation that will change after unification, allowing Korea to redirect its defense effort in ways that could concern Japan. Japanese may fear that a united Korea will be aggressively nationalistic, anti-Japa-nese, and free of the restraint imposed by the DPRK menace and the U.S. alliance.[27] Therefore, the need for a U.S. umbrella to "protect" Korea and Japan from each other will be greater after unification. These concerns may be irrational, but this does not make them less potent.

Besides the need to deploy the U.S. military in Asia for the sake of Japan-Korea relations, supporters of American deployment further reject the idea that because Japan is an economic super-power it can increase its military strength to compensate for a po-tential American drawdown, allowing the United States to save money by disbanding forces now in Asia. On paper, Japan has the resources to become the "policeman of Asia." Despite its economic problems, it has a GDP of almost $4 trillion, a strong industrial and technological base, a well-educated population, and a stable political system. It is unlikely, however, that it could replace the United States as the main provider of regional security, at least on the 2010–2015 horizon, unless there are cataclysmic changes.

First, almost no one in Japan wants the country to take the leading role in managing Asia. Japan's experience with the military convinced many Japanese that it was the road to disaster and made them allergic to the armed forces (many have drawn the wrong les-son: they see military power as intrinsically evil, failing to understand

---

27. This is a point that many Japanese analysts and officials made to the author during discussions in Tokyo in 1998 and 1999.

that it was soldiers and guns, not unilateral disarmament and confidence-building measures, that made it possible to unseat the Nazis and the Japanese militarists and deter the Soviets). Some Japanese want greater Japanese influence overseas and a more equal U.S.–Japan alliance, but assuming the sort of responsibilities the United States has taken upon itself is not what Japanese leaders, or voters, want. Replacing the United States would inevitably entail a large increase in the SDF, along with threatening other countries from time to time with military action and ordering the SDF into combat even in cases where there is no direct threat to Japan. Unless there are revolutionary changes, it is difficult to imagine a Japanese prime minister appearing on TV and saying that if country X does not stop its activities in some regional conflict not directly involving Japan, the Air Self-Defense Forces will bomb it into submission; the Maritime Self-Defense Forces will blockade it; and the Ground Self-Defense Forces will invade it. In addition, no Asian country, including Korea, desires such an expansion of Japan's security role because of memories of pre-1945 Japan and a fear that Japan's economic strength, if combined with military power and ambition, could subject Asia to Japanese domination. Anti-Japanese feelings will probably gradually subside in Asia, but the process will be slow and some residual fear of Japan will remain, if only because of Japan's wealth.

Second, Japan's politics shows the symptoms of what Maruyama Masao called "the system of irresponsibilities,"[28] where responsibility for decisions is so diffused that no individual or institution is in charge. This is not a new problem. Since the demise of the founding oligarchs in the early 20th century, Japan has had to live without an effective decision-making center, one of the reasons for its diplomatic failures in the 1930s and early 1940s and its inability to prosecute the war successfully. Despite recent improvements, the country's decision-making apparatus is not yet adapted to running the national security policy of an activist regional superpower. The prime minister's office is weak, staffed with officials who often represent the interests of the vari-

---

28. Chalmers Johnson, "The People Who Invested the Mechanical Nightingale," in Carol Gluck and Stephen R. Graubard, eds., *Showa: The Japan of Hirohito*, p. 74. See also George R. Packard III, *Protest in Tokyo*, p. 349.

ous bureaucracies, rather than helping the prime minister impose his will on the government. The practice of shadow decision-makers without formal positions further complicates the policy process and makes it harder to take quick or controversial actions. Implementing decisions is also undermined by the absence of a powerful SDF Joint Staff, a lack of SDF experience combined operations, and an ineffective interagency process.

Postwar Japan has had a very successful national security policy because Tokyo delegated a portion of it to the United States, freeing Japan from leading in defense matters. This has been beneficial to both Japan and the United States. Japan has avoided entanglements in military confrontations that would have soured its relations with Asia and divided itself at home. The United States, for its part, gets Japan's support to use Japanese bases, the cooperation of the SDF, and financial assistance to establish a peaceful international order in Northeast Asia. This arrangement has greatly benefited the United States, which profits so much from Asian peace and prosperity. But Japan would need to completely restructure its decision-making system to become Asia's political and military leader if the United States left the scene.

Third, Japan's isolation mitigates against a role as security leader. Because of its geography, it kept out of the major Cold War crises and, unlike Europe, was not at the heart of the Soviet-American confrontation, never having to send troops overseas and insulated by the sea from its adversaries. Its ties to the United States have been far more shallow than those of Germany, America's primary European ally. Japan did not experience a full U.S. military occupation government because General MacArthur reigned through the Japanese government, which administered the country. During the Cold War, Japan had far fewer American servicemen on its soil relative to its population than Germany or Korea (in addition, most were on Okinawa, not on the home islands). Its armed forces, unlike those of NATO states, have not been as closely integrated with those of the United States or other nations. Consequently, Japanese political and military leaders have very little experience in international political and security relations compared with their U.S. and European counterparts.

Furthermore, Japan remains culturally isolated. Except for some Koreans, Taiwanese, and Japanologists, virtually nobody is well-versed in the language, literature, and culture of Japan. Save for a few experts, even basic knowledge of Japanese politics and history is almost nonexistent outside Japan. And though Japan has become more international, the number of Japanese who are really familiar with foreign cultures and mores is small. This isolation would further hamper a Japanese attempt to become a leader in political and military affairs.

In addition, it is helpful for a state that wishes to lead to have ideological underpinnings to motivate its government and population. For Americans, it is the quest to export U.S. values to the rest of the world. Britain, in its imperial heyday, also had a sense of mission, as did other powers, from Spain in the 15th century to Japan in the pre-1945 era. Japan, at this point, probably lacks a motivating ideology to support a regional power role. The Liberal Democratic Party (LDP) has been very nonideological, focusing on delivering the goods and getting the votes.[29] For example, during the Security Treaty Crisis of 1960, the LDP government showed very little interest in the defense of the free world, collective security against communism, or preserving democracy.[30] Lacking a grand design is not necessarily bad; it has served Japan much better than the adventurism of the early Showa decades, but it makes it more difficult for Japan to be a strong actor in security affairs.

Also, Japan is aging rapidly. Its birthrate is far lower than that of the United States: Japan's fertility rate is about 1.48 per woman (compare with 2.07 in the United States),[31] and it has almost no immigration to fill the gap. Technology and improvements in health care make it possible for older individuals to contribute to the economy and to national defense. Nevertheless, for economic and psychological reasons, older nations may lack the dynamism that is required to assume a political and military lead-

---

29. See Tamamoto Masaru, "The Ideology of Nothingness," *World Policy Journal,* Spring 1994, pp. 89–99.

30. George R. Packard III, *Protest in Tokyo*, pp. 334–40.

31. See 1999 data, U.S. Census Bureau, http://www.census.gov/ipc/www/idbprint.html and http://www.census.gov/cgi-bin/ipc/idbsprd.

ership role. The supply of young men, who despite technology remain the backbone of any military, will also decline due to the low birth rate.

Another obstacle to Japan replacing the United States is that the SDF force structure is based on the assumption that the armed forces of the United States will participate in Japan's defense.[32] The United States provides long-range sensors (though Japan is thinking of launching reconnaissance satellites), intelligence, nuclear deterrence, and some naval and air support. Japan would have to revise its force structure drastically, as well as augment it, if the U.S. armed forces were taken out of the equation. It would have to build some areas of the SDF almost from scratch to compensate for an American withdrawal and to acquire force-projection capabilities to mount expeditionary wars. This is not an impossible task, but it would require an incompressible amount of time to train large numbers of enlisted men and officers, and hundreds of billions of dollars or more of additional defense spending.

Therefore, unless there is a political earthquake, Japan cannot be an alternative to the United States as the primary provider of military security in the region, at least for a couple of decades. Given the potential for Korean-Japanese, Sino-Japanese, Sino-Russian, Russian-Japanese, Russian-Korean, and Sino-Taiwanese tensions and other potential contingencies, it would be highly dangerous for the United States to abdicate its Asian responsibilities. (This situation is not unique to Asia. Absent the United States, the European Union is still incapable of sustaining stability in Europe.)

Moreover, the military component of the alliance between the United States and Japan performs an important task in enhancing the political cohesion of the U.S.–Japan alliance. It guarantees the United States some input into Japanese policy due to the major contribution the United States makes to Japanese security. It also gives Tokyo some influence over American policy because the United States requires Japanese cooperation, given American reliance on Japan as the pillar of its Asia policy. Without this

---

32. See Norm Levin's chapter in Zalmay Khalizad, ed., *Strategic Appraisal, 1996.*

link, Washington and Tokyo would have fewer reasons to pursue compatible policies and would run the risk of developing divergent strategies.

The arguments of those who favor a U.S. withdrawal or a gradual reduction in the size of the USFJ is based on several assumptions that lead them to believe such a course of action is desirable.

First, North Korea's demise will end the major military threat to the region, and thus the requirement for allied military power in the region will fall dramatically. There will be no need for Japan to "replace" the United States because the task of the U.S. military, i.e., deterring North Korea, will not need to be performed once North Korea is gone.

Second, even without U.S. military deployment in Asia, the combination of America's residual power in Asia, because of its superpower status and wealth, the economic self-interest of Asian nations, and the absence of major territorial rivalries will mean that Japan will not need to increase its armed forces significantly. Intra-Asian relations are far less adversarial than they were when the 1953 armistice was signed, especially those between Korea and Japan. Moreover, the U.S. economic presence in Asia will partly compensate for a lower military profile.

Third, Japan can strengthen its military if it wishes to do so. It is true that a major defense buildup would face many obstacles, but Japan does not need to develop into a superpower like the United States. Gradual increases, which could be undertaken with American help, would be sufficient because Japan does not face any powerful foes. China is still a Third World country, and all other states in the region are either fairly small or weak. Because there are no emergencies on the horizon, Japan can take one or two decades to gradually enhance its military stature and thus move at a pace it can handle without trauma.

Also, Japan has changed. It has gradually developed a broader interpretation of its constitution. SDF units have been participating in peacekeeping operations (Golan Heights, Mozambique, and Cambodia), and in March 1999, vessels of the Maritime Safety Agency and Maritime Self-Defense Forces fired live ammunition at a suspected North Korean spy ship. The Guideline Review process indicates a willingness to deepen the military relationship with the United States. The prime minister's office now has a crisis-management cell. Thus, one should not underestimate the ability of Japan to slowly assume a stronger role in regional affairs. Japanese leaders successfully dealt with national security emergencies and catastrophes in the Meiji era, when the country's sovereignty was at risk, and in 1945 when the nation had been bombed into rubble. Handling a U.S. withdrawal would be far less difficult than saving the empire from foreign subjugation in the second half of the 19ᵗʰ century or rebuilding the country after August 1945.

Concerning the U.S. bases in Japan, if the United States requires the use of facilities in Japan it can always use them when needed without keeping forces there on a permanent basis. There are, for example, no permanent U.S. installations in France, but U.S. planes were stationed in France during the Kosovo War of 1999.

American bases can also lead to anti-Americanism, especially in a situation where there are no obvious threats to Japan that justify depriving Japanese citizens of scarce land and forcing them to bear the social costs of hosting tens of thousands of foreign servicemen and noisy aircraft. Therefore, removing these facilities will eliminate an element of friction between the two countries and lead to an improved climate in U.S.–Japan relations.

According to this line of reasoning, there is no need for Japan to significantly enhance its military and diplomatic profile to compensate for a smaller American presence. A good relationship with the United States, and decent relations with Korea and possibly China, will be enough to keep Asia stabilized.

JAPANESE-KOREAN RELATIONS

Japanese-Korean relations have improved under the presidency of Kim Dae Jung. The Japanese government statement, issued jointly with that of the ROK during President Kim's visit to Tokyo in October 1998, was a major breakthrough in Korean-Japanese reconciliation. The Japanese apology for Japan's activities during the colonial era was unambiguous and issued as a clear statement of government policy. At the same time, President Kim wishes to go forward and build good relations across the Tsushima Strait rather than dwell on past suffering. The economic crisis in

Korea has also increased Korean interest in improving ties with Japan, while the North Korean missile program has made more Japanese policy-makers aware of the need for a closer relationship with South Korea.

Unfortunately, Japanese-Korean relations carry a heavy baggage of mistrust that will not evaporate in just a few years. Koreans remain bitter over the sufferings of the occupation period and have not forgotten the Japanese invasion of the late 16th century under Hideyoshi. Given this historical background, Korea, or at least some Koreans, tend to ascribe dark motives to Japanese policy. Moreover, conservative Japanese politicians are wont to make remarks, such as accusing the comfort women of being willing prostitutes or saying that Japan liberated Asia in the 1930s and 1940s, that inflame anti-Japanese feelings in Korea.

The Korean suspicion of Japan was visible during the North Korean spy ship incident off the coast of Japan in March 1999. The response of the Japanese Maritime Safety Agency and the Maritime Self-Defense Forces to an incursion by suspected North Korean intelligence or covert operation vessels was rather tame. The Japanese ships fired warning shots but did not use any coercive measures, such as targeting the vessels themselves or ramming them, and let them escape. The ROK government supported Japan's actions, but the public reaction in South Korea to this development was one of concern about possible Japanese militarism.

Moreover, during and after unification Korea will be weakened by the strain of unification and could feel vulnerable. With no Northern threat left, Koreans might focus on the perceived "Japanese menace," while some Japanese may see a unified Korea as a danger to Japan, with Korean and Japanese anxieties reinforcing each other. Several Japanese analysts interviewed for this project expressed fears that Korean nationalism would become anti-Japanese after unification. In particular, the immediate post-unification period could create new sources of conflict. Koreans may accuse Japan of not providing enough aid for unification and request an assistance package to compensate northern Korea for the damages of Japanese occupation (assuming that this issue did not get resolved while the DPRK existed). There may also be resentment at Japanese foreign investment in northern Korea if Koreans think that "Japanese are buying Korea." (This reaction was found in the United States in the 1980s during the buying spree of Japanese investors in the United States. Given that Japan is much bigger relative to Korea than to the United States, it would be understandable if these reactions developed in Korea.)

Korea after unification will still be a small country surrounded by two continent-size nuclear powers, China and the Russian Federation, and an economic superpower, Japan. In addition, some Koreans consider Japan a "semi–nuclear power" because it possesses the capability to develop nuclear weapons and ballistic missiles quickly.[33] Two other Asian states, India and Pakistan, are armed with nuclear bombs and missiles. Thus, some Korean politicians may argue that a unified Korea should keep the North's missile and nuclear programs because not to do so would leave Korea unilaterally disarmed against China, Russia, and Japan.[34] They could also note that India and Pakistan, two nations well below Korea in economic and technological achievements, did not suffer much diplomatically or economically by going nuclear. Korean nuclearization, even if limited to discussions, would frighten Japanese because Japan lacks a nuclear deterrent, and it is easy to imagine how just a few extremist anti-Japanese Korean propagandists could cause great alarm in Japan.[35]

Thus, the United States should keep forces in both nations to prevent Japanese-Korean tensions by "protecting" them from one another. The United States can also act as a catalyst to foster Japanese-Korean military cooperation and thus improve relations between these two American allies.

Another argument in favor of a continued U.S. presence in Korea is that only a strong U.S. military presence can convince Koreans that, in exchange for a continued credible American commitment, the ROK should not develop long-range missiles and nuclear warheads. A nuclear-armed Korea would not be a threat to

---

33. See T. W. Kim, "South Korean's Nuclear Dilemmas," *Korea and World Affairs* 16 (summer 1992), pp. 250–93, for this line of argument, Japan being already "a semi–nuclear power" and Korea basically surrounded by nuclear power, p. 254.

34. See C. S. Eliot Kang, "Korean Unification: A Pandora's Box of Northeast Asia," *Asian Perspective* 20, no. 2 (fall-winter 1996), pp. 9–43.

35. See Mike M. Mochizuki, *Japan: Domestic Change and Foreign Policy*, p. 80.

the United States, but it would open the door, as noted above, for a competitive arms race in the region that would wreak havoc on Japanese-Korean relations.

An alternative evaluation of Korean-Japanese ties is that although no one would claim that Japanese-Korean relations are perfect, the existing animosity is unlikely to degenerate into anything destabilizing. Japan has no interest in reconquering Korea. Save for TokDo[36] (Takeshima in Japanese and Liancourt Rocks in English), about which the vast majority of Japanese care very little, there are no territorial disputes. Even the TokDo controversy is not explosive, because Korea controls the islets and it is unthinkable that the Japanese government would ever use force to alter the status quo. As for Korea, it is not about to embark on a reenactment of the 13th century invasion of Japan (by the Mongols) from Korea. The comfort women issue will vanish as the victims die of old age. In addition, Korea needs Japanese technology and capital and thus cannot afford to antagonize Japan. There may be strong antagonisms, but these have not prevented the development of economic and political ties (as has happened in the Netherlands, for example, where latent hostility to Germany remains virulent but does not impede close cooperation with Germany, including monetary union). Moreover, after unification Koreans will have to devote all their energy during the following decades to domestic issues. A unified Korea will be a nation primarily absorbed by its own internal challenges rather than an active player in international relations.

Thus, if one is more optimistic about the future of Japanese-Korean relations, the argument that U.S. forces should stay is less persuasive. Therefore, in this view, there will be no requirement for American military forces to remain in the region for the sake of maintaining amicable Korean-Japanese relations.

SINO-JAPANESE RELATIONS

It is undiplomatic for the Japanese government to openly voice too much concern about China. The atrocities perpetrated

---

36. Islets located between Japan and Korea. Both countries claim them but they are under ROK control.

by the Imperial Japanese Army in China during the War of 1937–1945, China's size, and Japan's reluctance to take controversial positions, all militate in favor of not branding China an enemy. Below the surface, however, Japan has doubts about China. As several analysts and officials interviewed for this study noted, many Japanese policy-makers are concerned about China's ambitions. In recent years, Beijing has often done its best to fuel Japanese suspicions. It continued nuclear tests for many years while receiving Japanese aid; it fired missiles close to Taiwan, threatening a country that is probably Japan's only true friend in the region (Taiwanese, who have fond memories of Japanese colonialism, are the only naturally pro-Japanese Northeast Asians); and it claims Japanese territory (Sengaku islands, Daioyutai in Chinese) as it tries to gain control of South China Sea islands as far south as Indonesian waters. China has not been helpful in dealing with North Korea, shrouding its relations with Pyongyang in secrecy and eschewing participation in the Agreed Framework. China has also vociferously opposed ballistic missile defense, whereas many Japanese believe that in light of the North Korean rocket program it is incumbent on Japan to develop a missile shield, especially because their country lacks a nuclear deterrent of its own. Moreover, China's diplomatic style is extremely different from Japan's. Japanese officials always avoid aggressive statements, but China's rulers are wont to hurl verbal abuse at foreign governments and their own people.

Apart from these issues, there is an undercurrent of concern about China's long-term goals. Since Japan's emergence from seclusion, Japan and China have fought two wars, and though the People's Republic is not a modern country, many Japanese suspect it of hegemonic ambitions. As long as Russia lingers in its enfeebled state, China is the only Asian power that can become a major long-term threat to Japanese security.

The division of Korea has attenuated Japanese-Chinese rivalry in Asia. The DPRK has provided China with a solid barrier against Japanese inroads on the Asian mainland. For Japan, the ROK and U.S. armies in Korea ensure that China will not attempt to control the entire Peninsula as it did in 1950, and earlier, during the Yuan (Mongol) monarchy, and under the Ming and the late Qing dynasties. Unification could change the situation by removing the twin buffers of North Korea and the U.S. Army in Korea that separate China from Japan.

Following Korean unification, unless China has dramatically changed it will seek to enhance its influence in Korea, and this could possibly lead to Japanese actions to counter the Chinese "advance" into Korea. At the beginning, this would probably be only a relatively benign quest for political and economic advantage, but it could gradually evolve into a much more malign confrontation. In addition, Korean factions could be engulfed in the rivalry, with some supporting China and others Japan, thus undermining Korea's stability. Russia could also become involved, but it is unclear which side it would support.

A Sino-Japanese dispute over Korea would develop into a broader confrontation for supremacy in Asia. China might wish to establish hegemony on the mainland and exclude Japanese influence from the continent. This could lead to different outcomes. One would be a vassalization of Japan resulting from what Charles Horner called the achievement of China's ultimate goal of "restoring" the "historical balance" of Sino-Japanese relations.[37] Japan would succumb because of its unwillingness to fight for its interests, its aging population, and its petrified political system. This would deprive the United States of its most important ally and allow China to exert a predominant influence on Japan. United States power would be eliminated from East Asia, which would be absorbed into a Chinese empire, and America's position as the world's sole superpower would end. This would be the worst strategic setback for the United States since the breakup of the Union in 1861. This development would also hurt Asia's economy because a Chinese-dominated Asia would be hostile to free enterprise. Subjugation of Japan is, however, an almost impossible scenario.

The other possibility—that Japan would replace the United States as the regional hegemon by completely knocking out China from the competition—is also low, but less so than Chinese victory. Japan does have many advantages. The Japanese polity is far stronger than the Chinese because it rests on a stable middle class

---

37. Charles Horner, "Rising Sun, the Good Earth, and the U.S.," *The National Interest* (fall 1996), p. 6.

and a political system that is accepted by the vast majority of the population. In addition, Japan is technologically well ahead of China and has a well-educated population that could be mobilized to create a great war machine. China, as mentioned later, suffers from a host of debilitating challenges that will prevent it from becoming a great power and may well lead to a collapse of the regime.

But even though Japan could defeat attempts at Chinese hegemony, it is most unlikely that it could become powerful enough to dominate China, because of the handicaps mentioned in the previous section. Frequent crises in the region, over Korea, Taiwan, the Sengaku islands, and other potential flash points, could occur between China and Japan. Japan's political and technological superiority would not be sufficient to overwhelm China, whose size and geographic location would allow it to retain nuisance value, unless China were to break into several pieces (in which case civil war in China would be a problem). Sino-Japanese tensions could also have serious repercussions for the development of China if the Communist Party loses power. A post-communist China will not necessarily be a nonnationalistic China. If relations with Japan were already bad, it is possible that demagogues and xenophobes could exploit these tensions for domestic purposes and pursue an anti-Japanese course after the overthrow of the communist regime.

Japan would most likely acquire nuclear weapons (or more sophisticated arms yet to be invented), with ICBMs (or their successors) as delivery vehicles to deter China. (Even if ballistic missile defense is operational, it is unlikely to provide 100 percent reliability and to be deemed sufficiently effective to spare Japan from fielding at least a nuclear retaliatory capability to deter China.) Nuclear Japan, in the context of a U.S. withdrawal from Asia, would be a positive development for the United States because it would be a sign of Japan's unwillingness to kowtow to China. This probable acquisition of nuclear weapons could, however, undermine U.S.–Japanese ties because of the American anti-proliferation lobby's opposition. The United States has, under several administrations, been willing to put significant pressure on its allies and friends over proliferation (South Korea, Taiwan, Brazil, and Argentina) or the transfer of nuclear technology to third parties (Germany and France), even at the risk of harming relations with allied nations. Therefore, Japan's development of nuclear weapons could lead to a major deterioration of U.S.–Japanese ties. South Korea caved in to the United States on the nuclear issue because it was much more vulnerable to U.S. pressure and could trust the credibility of the U.S. deterrent, thanks to the American army division and U.S. tactical air units on its soil. Japan, with a much bigger economy and with no U.S. forces, would have no incentive to give in to Washington if it thought that the United States has abandoned it. Moreover, China would try to foster anti-Japanese sentiment in the United States by portraying Japan as an imperialist state bent on the same anti-Chinese and anti-American aggression as occurred in the 1930s.

Even if Japanese-American relations survived the nuclearization of Japan, the situation in East Asia would be destabilized. Japan's domestic politics would be at risk of being shattered by divisions over defense. Korea would almost surely be horrified by Japan's nuclearization and acquire nuclear weapons itself, and it would perhaps seek military ties with China. Other Asian states, such as Singapore or Australia, might also react adversely.

There is admittedly a small probability that Chinese imperialism could lead to the creation of a Japan-led coalition, with Korea, Taiwan, and maybe Russia, and supported by the United States. Such a development, however, is highly improbable. It would require a radical transformation of Japan's domestic political system, and also imply that Korea and other Asian states would willingly become Japan's junior partners.

Sino-Japanese rivalry could at worst degenerate into a war on a scale not seen since 1945: Japan, Korea, Taiwan, and China have large populations and economies and the technology to build and buy advanced weaponry. Therefore, an arms race in the region would create the potential for conflagrations on the scale of a world war.

Pessimists who are concerned about Sino-Japanese relations see the U.S. military presence as essential to forestall Sino-Japanese rivalry. In this view, U.S. armed forces are needed in Asia regardless of what happens to North Korea because unless the U.S.–ROK–Japan military triangle is powerful, there are great risks that Sino-Japanese hostility, rather than U.S.–led stability, would be the defining aspect of Asian affairs.

Optimists look at Sino-Japanese relations differently. They note that Japan has totally changed since the 1930s. It is a pacifist democracy without any of the expansionist and militaristic tendencies of the past. China has evolved as well; it has started to develop a middle class, is far freer than it was 20 years ago, and aspires to growth, not war. In spite of its sometimes violent rhetoric, the Chinese government is well aware that few nations are as peaceful as Japan. It also knows that China needs Japanese investment and trade to thrive. Despite the horrors of the past, Asians admire Japan, and young people, including South Koreans, are drawn to its pop culture and consumer brands.

Moreover, the international situation has changed. When Japan took over Korea, it feared European and American imperialism and thought Japan must conquer or die. Under the Meiji ruler, Japan sought to develop its economy through political control of overseas markets, as others were doing.[38] Today nobody needs to own a country to sell to it. In the Imperial era there was also a desire in Japan to acquire land overseas to settle its demographic surplus, whereas no one in contemporary Japan believes in settlement colonies for Japan's declining and aging population. Finally, the importance of Korea and China to Japan's foreign trade has diminished considerably compared to the pre–World War II era, when China, Taiwan, and Korea (then colonies or under Japanese influence) accounted for a larger proportion of Japanese trade than today (30 percent in 1913, 40 percent in 1936, 23 percent in 1996).[39] Even if Korea fell under Chinese influence, it would continue to trade with Japan, as Hong Kong does, and the impact on Japan would be limited. Militarily, Korea is not a "dagger at the heart of Japan" simply because military technology makes distance far less relevant. ICBMs in western China are no less lethal than those in silos in Pusan. On the Chinese side, the People's Republic has shown more interest in commerce than in overseas expansion. In addition, Korea is infinitely stronger than it was in the late 19th century and would not be easy prey to either China or Japan.

---

38. See Albert Craig et al., East Asia.

39. See statistics in Barry Turner, ed., *The Statesman's Year-Book 1998–1999*, p. 829, and William W. Lockwood, *The Economic Development of Japan*, p. 395 (imports and exports).

Thus, optimistic observers believe that Japan and China will develop a symbiotic economic relationship, merging China's labor and size with Japanese technology and capital, as the United States and Mexico have done along the Rio Grande. Economic cooperation is more likely than political and military confrontation between Asia's two large powers. A powerful U.S. military in Asia would heighten Chinese fears of American containment, put Korea in a difficult situation between hostile blocs, and possibly push Japan toward a higher military profile within the U.S. military alliance. With the removal of North Korea, the threat of war in Asia will diminish greatly and American forces will be at best superfluous and at worst nefarious.

SINO-KOREAN RELATIONS

Following unification, China will share a border with a U.S.–allied liberal democracy. Since there are about two million ethnic Korean Chinese citizens on the Chinese side of the border in Manchuria (Jilin province), this new border would add to Beijing's concerns about Korea because the Korean-Chinese might become more attracted to Korea (right now, the horrible state of affairs in North Korea must make them happy that they are Chinese rather than North Koreans). Chinese anxiety over Manchuria might also be fueled by the fact that some Koreans consider parts of southern Manchuria as Korean territory that was unlawfully ceded by Japan to China during the colonial era (some South Korean textbooks say as much).[40]

Depending on the process of unification, China might intervene in the North to "restore order" near the Chinese border. Chinese intervention in northern North Korea might be welcomed by Seoul if there is an outbreak of violent anarchy in the North and the ROK is overwhelmed by the demands on its army, police, and relief services. But China might overstay its welcome or could seek to impose conditions that are detrimental to ROK sovereignty. It might, for instance, press for limits on ROK (and U.S., if any) forces in the north, as well as for greater unilateral authority on

40. Korean Ministry of Education, *Korean History for Ethnic Koreans Abroad*, p. 256.

the Yalu, the right to pursue Chinese citizens who cross the border, or special rights of access to some Korean ports on the Sea of Japan (known as the East Sea in Korea). China may also place agents in Korea during the period of collapse in the North. Even if China does not intervene in North Korea during the regime's breakdown, it might try to achieve some of these goals through covert operations and diplomatic and economic pressure.

The history of Communist China's relations with neighboring states bodes ill for post-unification Sino-Korean relations. The PRC has attacked numerous neighbors or encroached on their territories—small ones such as Vietnam and the Philippines and large ones such as India and the Soviet Union. Following its absorption of Hong Kong, it has undermined the territory's autonomy by trying its residents in China for crimes committed in the territory and by expressing its opposition to Hong Kong court rulings. Consequently, it is likely that following the demise of North Korea, the Chinese government will seek to expand its influence on the Korean Peninsula. It is difficult to believe that China could treat Korea as an equal partner, since for many centuries Korea was a tributary state of China (even though in practice it was independent). In addition, China's communist government has always had a confrontational attitude toward international relations, and China is 43 times larger and 18 times more populous than unified Korea.

Aggressive Chinese interest in a united Korea could have different outcomes. Chinese influence could predominate, thanks to China's strength and proximity and the absence of a countervailing force if the U.S. presence were withdrawn (with Japan being too weak militarily and too distrusted by Koreans to balance Chinese influence, and Russia unlikely to be strong enough for several decades). Such a development, however, would not be immediate and would create tensions within Korea because many Korean nationalists would oppose China. If, in the long run, China were successful, it would deprive the United States of its only continental Asian ally. It would also worsen Sino-Japanese relations because Japan would feel threatened. The United States could retreat to a "Fortress Japan" position in Asia, but this would undermine American credibility in Japan: the United States would be blamed for "losing Korea" to China, and many Japanese would doubt the willingness of the United States to honor its commitment to defend Japan.

Alternatively, Korea could halt Chinese encroachment with Japanese backing if Japan and Korea became military allies. This would be a much better outcome for the United States but, as noted, it would require a very dramatic transformation of Korean-Japanese relations and of Japanese security policy. Moreover, it would lead to increased tension in Asia because of the rise in Sino-Japanese hostility. A Japanese alliance would also be more divisive in Korea than reliance on the United States. Therefore, even if China did not manage to extend its sphere of influence to Korea, it is likely that Korean factions, helped by Beijing, would seek to derail the development of a Korean-Japanese partnership.

Thus, possible Korean-Chinese disputes are one of the justifications for maintaining the U.S. presence in Korea. By making it clear that Korea remains in the U.S. defense perimeter, the United States will deter China from attempting to bring Korea under Chinese influence and thus hinder the rise of Sino-Korean (and Sino-Japanese) hostility. Preventing such tensions will also contribute to Korea's internal stability because a Chinese quest for hegemony, successful or not, would lead to internal divisions in Korea.

Optimists take a different approach to the possibility of Korean-Chinese tension. They note that neither China nor Korea has territorial claims on the other. The Korean-Chinese are not an oppressed minority like the Tibetans and the Uigurs. They enjoy a higher socioeconomic status than the Han and are well integrated into Chinese society. They have no reason to be anti-Han, and there are no Korean-Chinese Dalai Lamas or mullahs. Unlike the Turkic Muslims and Tibetans, Korean-Chinese live in a sea of Han Chinese, not in remote colonial provinces, making secession impossible. The Chinese admire the ROK and are not hostile to it, and they respect Koreans for their industriousness. Some Koreans may think that Manchuria is part of their homeland, but no Korean president is going to launch a crusade to reconquer it. Korea has almost no ethnic Chinese, who are sometimes a source of tension between China and its neighbors, and Koreans readily admit the cultural debt they owe Chinese civilization, which they generally admire.

Not only will Korea be strong enough to avoid becoming a satellite of China, but China has no interest in achieving such a goal. Rather, a stable and prosperous Korea appeals to China because Korea will be a market for Chinese goods and a source of foreign investment. China would be far worse off if it tried to control Korea, generating an anti-Chinese reaction. Even in the case of Taiwan—an island the Chinese rulers consider an integral part of the People's Republic—pragmatism has prevailed, with China doing brisk business with the Taiwanese.

In this optimistic projection, American soldiers would harm the development of good Sino-Korean ties after unification, because Beijing would perceive Korea as a hostile U.S. base. As long as the DPRK remains a menace, Chinese leaders see the need for a U.S. presence to deter the North; but after unification, any remaining U.S. force will be seen as an anti-Chinese foothold on the mainland. Maintaining U.S. forces in a country bordering China would thus be a provocation. America's goal should be to foster friendly Sino-Korean relations as part of a peaceful order in Northeast Asia rather than to erect barriers against China in Korea.

There is yet another perspective on Sino-Korean ties. America is more than 8,000 kilometers from Korea, whereas China is across the river. China has more than a billion citizens, a growing economy, and more at stake in Korea than the United States. Therefore, it is no more realistic for the United States to deny Korea to China than for China to dominate Mexico. The United States should therefore be willing to accept Chinese hegemony in Korea and rely on a set of maritime alliances with Japan and Australia. Korea, according to this analysis, is not vital to the United States. Its economy is relatively small (about $300 billion vs. $3,200 billion for Japan)[41] and its military potential is limited. In addition, the United States has had unpleasant experiences with land wars on the Asian mainland (Korea, Vietnam). Korean unification will provide the opportunity for the United States to extract itself from the risk of ground fighting in Asia. Therefore, regardless of Chinese intentions in Korea, it makes no sense for the United States

---

41. The Economist, *The World in 1999*, p. 75

to expend energy and risk confrontation with China over the Peninsula.

CHINA'S FOREIGN POLICY

There are different perspectives on the foreign policy of China. One view is communist China as an aggressive country. Going back to the Korean War, research indicates that the intervention of the People's Republic was planned before MacArthur crossed the 38th parallel and had far more expansionist aims than defending Manchuria from the Americans, including possibly assisting North Korea in occupying all of the Peninsula.[42] The PRC has been bellicose toward Taiwan, invaded Tibet, and, as noted earlier, attacked several neighbors (and even prior to the communist takeover, China, like all successful empires, took over territories to expand its realm, despite its claims that it has never been expansionist). Observing contemporary China's behavior, one notes that "Hyper-sovereignty values are still a central drive of Chinese foreign policy."[43] Furthermore, unlike many Americans who believe in "win-win" situations, Chinese strategists practice zero-sum games,[44] as demonstrated by Beijing's unwillingness to participate in multilateral efforts to defuse the North Korean nuclear problem or to resolve the maritime boundary questions in the South China Sea.

Once Korea is unified, China will not tolerate the USFK, which is only useful as long as there is a North Korea. Given China's attitude toward the United States, China will then want to end the USFK presence after unification and may seek the abrogation of

---

42. See Chen Jian, *China's Road to the Korean War*, pp. 158—159, and Zhang Shu Guang, *Mao's Military Romanticism*, p. 85, and Woodrow Wilson International Center for Scholars, Cold War International History Project Bulletin no. 6-7, *The Cold War in Asia*, Kathryn Weathersby "New Russian Documents on the Korean War," p. 34.

43. Alastair I. Johnston, "China's Militarized Interstate Dispute Behavior 1949–1992: A First Cut at the Data," *China Quarterly* no. 153 (March 1998), p. 2.

44. See David M. Finkelstein, "China's National Military Strategy," in *The People's Liberation Army in the Information Age,* James C. Mulvenon and Richard H. Yang, editors.

the U.S.–ROK alliance. The recently published Chinese government Defense White Paper[45] is abstruse, but explains that China opposes the U.S. alliance system in Northeast Asia. In addition to its official documents, China's policies in the past 10 years indicate that it takes a dim view of American defense policy in Asia. It has opposed the strengthening of the U.S.–Japan Alliance and made noises against ballistic missile defense.

It is important to understand that the ruling party's opposition to the United States is rational. To the Communist Party, America is a malignant tumor. Its ethos is dedicated to the destruction of communism, and even if the U.S. administration is friendly to the People's Republic, American media, schools, clergymen, and politicians preach values that are antithetical to those of the party and that promote Tibetan secessionism, Taiwan independence, individualism, freedom of speech, political dissent, and religious upheaval. When President Clinton suggests "engaging" China to allow it to evolve, he is, probably unwittingly, declaring ideological war on the Chinese Communist Party; the entire logic of "engagement" is that it will cause China to become more like America—a worthy goal for Americans but not for the Chinese goverment. In addition, the United States sells weapons to Taiwan, and many Americans support Chinese dissidents who use the United States as a sanctuary. Because the United States is the largest market for Chinese goods and has the only educational system that can process the large numbers of students to whom China wants to give a modern education, the goverment cannot simply cut off ties with the United States. That does not mean, however, that China's leaders like the United States. It is probable that after Korean unification Beijing will try to eject U.S. military power from the Asian mainland because the United States is an inherently unfriendly partner for Beijing's rulers. For China, getting rid of the USFK will not stop all U.S. influence in Korea but, it will at least lessen it in a neighboring state. (Of course, if the Communist Party regime has been overthrown, the situation might be different, though post-communist might not automatically mean pro-American.) Therefore, the United States should realize that relations with China will be tense. China

---

45. Information Office of the State Council of the People's Republic of China, *China's National Defense*, July 1998, pp. 5–6.

needs the United States and may wish to avoid conflict, but there will be tensions. Moreover, China's growing integration into the world economy does not guarantee that it will seek peace. There was much international trade in Europe in 1914 but that did not prevent World War I. Given China's hostility, the United States should keep troops in Korea to make it clear to the PRC that the United States will not accept Chinese expansion in Northeast Asia. It is also a signal that the United States can be counted on by its allies.

Others take a more hopeful view of Sino-American relations and believe that as China's inexorable rise continues, the United States and China can coexist peacefully. *Living with China*, a book edited by Ezra Vogel (who predicted Japan's emergence as the world's leading economy), notes that China will continue to grow at unprecedented rates[46] but that the United States can reach accommodation with China, an opinion shared by many analysts who have been generally favorable to President Clinton's engagement of the PRC.

This school of thought sees China's growth as a challenge, but believes that the United States can successfully face it. China has not historically been an expansionist power,[47] and the Peoples' Liberation Army (PLA) is technologically backward and not capable of seriously threatening American interests. It also believes that China recognizes the benefits of America's military power in Asia. William Overholt of Nomura Securities noted that during informal discussions, "the Chinese have indicated a willingness to contemplate ... having an American division present" in Korea after unification.[48]

Such views lead to policy recommendations like those of *Strategic Assessment 1988*, a publication of the U.S. National

---

46. See Ezra Vogel, ed., *Living with China*.

47. William J. Dobson, Review of Richard Bernstein and Ross Munro's *"The Coming Conflict with China"* in *Survival* 34, no. 3 (summer 1997), p.164, and also Chen Jian, "The China Challenge in the Twenty-First Century: Implications of U.S. Foreign Policy," Washington, D.C.: United States Institute of Peace, June 1998.

48. William H. Overholt, "Korea: To the Market via Socialism," Singapore: BankBoston NA, *Emerging Markets Research: Asia*, 21 July 1998, no page number.

Defense University's Institute for National Strategic Studies (INSS), that advocates a "China as Full Member of the Core,"[49] or as others have proposed, giving it G-7 membership.[50] (an offer that China declined in February 2000 when the Japanese government invited it to join Okinawa summit). By engaging China, the United States can help China understand that U.S. military power, by keeping the peace, is good for China as well.[51] Though there are areas of disagreement, this analysis considers that on major issues, such as international stability, preserving free trade, and regional peace, China and the United States share the same goals despite occasional conflicts. In addition, China has been "responsible" and "helpful"[52] in the talks over North Korea. This reflects a liberal vision of world politics, where free markets and free trade are the best deterrents against war and where most nations are rational, as defined by sensible Americans, and share America's universal values.

To the extent that there are disputes between Washington and Beijing, these are either downplayed or blamed on others. Some see Taiwan's president as the cause of the tension in the Taiwan Straits.[53] The United States is also seen (at least partly) as responsible for Sino-American tensions, dating back to U.S. support for the Nationalists during the Chinese Civil War and extending to the decision to sell F-16 combat aircraft to Taiwan and al-

---

49. Hans Binnendijk, ed. in chief, *Strategic Assessment 1988*, p. 39 (principal author for Asia is Ronald N. Montaperto).

50. Robert B. Zoelick, "China: What Engagement Should Mean," *National Interest* no. 46 (winter 1996-7) p. 18. See also Chen Jian, "The China Challenge in the Twenty-First Century: Implications of U.S. Foreign Policy," Washington, D.C.: United States Institute of Peace, June 1998.

51. Robert B. Zoelick, "China: What Engagement Should Mean," *National Interest* no. 46 (winter 1996–97, p. 17–18).

52. Hans Binnendijk and Ronald N. Montaperto, eds., *Strategic Trend in China*, p. 119 (Ronald Montaperto).

53. See Hans Binnendijk, ed. in chief, *Strategic Assessment 1988*, p. 46 (principal author for Asia is Ronald N. Montaperto), and Chen Jian, "The China Challenge in the Twenty-First Century: Implications of U.S. Foreign Policy," Washington, D.C.: United States Institute of Peace, June 1998.

low President Lee Teng-hui to visit Cornell University. These analysts deplore the hostility toward China that developed in the United States after the Tiananmen massacre and note, quite accurately, that China's record on human rights has improved considerably in the past few decades.

Consequently, according to his vision of Sino-American relations, best illustrated by President Clinton's 1998 journey to the Middle Kingdom, China and America can work together in harmony most of the time and minimize conflict. The United States thus need not maintain large military forces in Asia to deal with a "Chinese threat," and too strong an American military deployment might actually be counterproductive because it would provoke China.

TAIWAN

Taiwan gained de facto independence when the Nationalist government (KMT or Kuomintang) retreated to the island following its defeat in the Civil War in 1949. For several decades, Communists and Nationalists refused to accept the reality of Taiwan's separation from China and called for reunification (though on different terms). As the mainland exiles have gradually lost influence on Taiwan, however, Taiwanese policy has changed, and the island has pursued a course of separation from China. Taiwan has also acquired a national identity that is partly Chinese but also uniquely Taiwanese. Taiwan survived the "derecognition" of its government by the United States thanks to Taiwan's economic dynamism, the ambiguous policy of the Beijing authorities toward the island, the Taiwan Relations Act (which Congress forced upon the Carter Administration), and the extended deterrence provided by American military power in the region. Taiwan's domestic transformation has had a big impact on its international position. In the days of the KMT dictatorship, Taiwan relied mostly on right-wing Republicans (the old China Lobby) for support in the United States. As Taiwan has become a pluralistic democracy, it has kept the support of anti-communist conservatives, but it has also built support among Democrats and political liberals. Taiwan has also benefited from China's move "to the right." The American left used to admire the Maoist regime, but since China has become semi-capitalist the American left has lost its zeal for promoting the PRC.

Some believe that Korean unification could induce China to seek its own "reunification" and invade Taiwan, especially if U.S. forces left Asia after Korean unification. Alternatively, Taiwan might acquire weapons of mass destruction to compensate for U.S. withdrawal from Asia and exchange technology with so-called rogue states, which would sell their know-how for money (of which Taiwan has a lot). Taiwan's nuclearization would not, in itself, be a threat to the United States. It would, however, increase Japanese worries about regional stability, which could in turn lead to an arms race involving China, Taiwan, Korea, and Japan, and a worsening of tensions in the region. The alleged beginning of some sort of Taiwanese–North Korean ties, including discussions of the storage of low-level nuclear waste, is an example of where Taiwanese insecurity might lead its government.

For some Americans, Taiwan's welfare is important. First, it is a free society that a dictatorship wants to annex, and the United States should help liberal democracies. Second, if the United States lets Taiwan down, it would damage the credibility of the U.S. defense commitment to its Asian allies. Third, a Sino-Taiwanese war would be highly detrimental to regional stability. It is thus better for the United States to face sporadic Chinese anger over America's support for Taiwan than to stop helping Taiwan and pay the much higher price of a full-fledged war between Taiwan and China, which could involve the United States. It makes sense for the United States to continue to extend indirect deterrence through U.S. bases and personnel in Korea and Japan. The stronger the United States is in the region, the more likely it is that there will be no doubt about American support for Taiwan and therefore no war.

Others have a different interpretation of the future of Sino-Taiwanese relations, because Taiwan and China are now major trade and investment partners. The Taiwanese have poured billions into the Chinese economy, and millions of Taiwanese have been to China on business or for tourism. Younger Taiwanese opposition politicians are less anti-mainland than their elders, recognizing the need to cohabit with China. As long as Taiwan does not formally declare independence, Sino-Taiwanese relations will remain peaceful.

China needs the capital and expertise of the Taiwanese, and Taiwanese businessmen want to build factories in China to escape Taiwan's high costs and declining tolerance for pollution, and to sell to the world's most populous marketplace. According to this view, the economic self-interest of both parties, not U.S. military power, prevents war between Taiwan and China.

Thus, from this perspective, there is no need to be overly concerned about Taiwan's fate. In addition, Korean unification will be a moral victory for the Taiwanese model (liberal democracy) against the Chinese one (communism) and will strengthen Taiwan's hand and its self-confidence. In some cases, the U.S. diplomatic and military activism makes things worse because Washington does not understand the subtleties of Sino-Taiwanese relations and prevents both sides from resolving their dispute by fostering anti–PRC elements in Taiwan who are emboldened by U.S. support. Therefore, the Taiwan problem does not require the continued presence of the U.S. military in Asia.

There is also a third school of thought. It is that China is very important to America's future and that Taiwan's welfare should not concern the United States. Consequently, what happens between Taiwan and China is not America's problem, and there is no reason for the United States to take it upon itself to protect Taiwan.

RUSSIA

Russia is not a major player in Asia at this time. There is always the possibility, however, of problems arising from Russia, such as disturbances in Vladivosk and the Maritime Provinces. China might at some point seek greater influence in the empty Russian spaces bordering China or want to gain control of a corridor from Manchuria to the Sea of Japan through Russian territory. Chinese migration into the Federation might cause conflict, as could disputes between Russian regions that want even closer ties to China and the central government.

The U.S. role in Northeast Asia is centered on the Japan-Korea-Taiwan area, and Russia is outside the core interests of the United States in Asia. Proponents of continued U.S. deployment would, however, argue that a powerful U.S. military in Asia can, to a very limited extent, mitigate the consequences of instability in the Russian Far East. The U.S. presence could create conditions for maintaining some military contacts, through Partnership-for-Peace type activities, with the Russian Far East. The United States might be able, up to a (limited) point, to influence Russian policy in Asia along lines favorable to the United States and its allies. Others would argue that Russia is so peripheral to Asian affairs that it should not influence U.S. policy in Asia.

U.S. FORCES IN NORTHEAST ASIA AFTER UNIFICATION

*I*n the preceding pages we have discussed the principal strategic issues that will confront the United States after Korean unification. Assuming that the United States retains forces in Korea after unification, it will need to decide how strong they should be and how they should be organized. There are several competing concepts regarding these questions. The positions that favor a large U.S. deployment after unification reflect a belief that post-unification Asia will still need U.S. military power to manage the potentially debilitating effect of regional tensions and maintain a strong U.S.-Japan-Korea triangle. Those who favor keeping only some token forces assume that once North Korea is eliminated there will be far fewer challenges to peace in Asia, or that if there are crises a strong U.S. presence is not the way to deal with them.

One line of thought is that Korean unification should be an opportunity to restructure, rather than reduce, the American military presence in Korea.[54] The United States would transform the USFK (which is currently not capable of deploying rapidly outside of Korea because its only military task is to defend the ROK) into a deployable force that could simultaneously be used to project

---

54. See Robert Odell, ed., *China, the United States, and Japan*, p. 42.

power as well as to protect Korea. This force could consist of two brigades: a heavy one with equipment at sea or positioned in other countries and a light one that could be deployed by air.

This would require moving the USFK to a location where it would be close to a large airport to provide rapid mobility. The air component of the USFK would be restructured, with more transports and fewer fighters. There would also be major changes in logistics intelligence and support functions to make the USFK capable of deploying forces outside the Peninsula. One argument in favor of this option is that the post-unification "shelf life" of the U.S. marines stationed in Japan is likely to be quite short after Korean unification, meaning that the U.S. Army in Korea would remain the only American land-power element in Northeast Asia. Therefore, the USFK after unification should be, if anything, more potent than it is today to compensate for the loss of U.S. manpower based in Japan and should assume the expeditionary role of the U.S. Marines based in Okinawa.

This transformation of the USFK would significantly raise the profile and influence of Korea in the United States. Korea would "graduate" from its status as just one ally to which the United States has an obligation to that of a real partner in regional affairs. Korea, which has historically been perceived as a recipient of U.S. security services (and by some as a burden), would become a provider of regional stability by hosting a U.S. regional force based in Korea. Its voice would carry much greater weight in Washington than it does today, because the United States would have to take into account Seoul's opinion, given America's reliance on a Korea-based U.S. force for Asian security.

This scheme could, however, also increase potential areas of friction between Korea and the United States. As the host of a large U.S. military force, Korea would seek more influence on U.S. policy and could sometimes oppose those actions that it felt were detrimental to its interests (for example, American support for Taiwan).

At the other extreme, the United States could retain its alliance with Korea but maintain almost no forces there, with the exception of some personnel to maintain access to facilities. This would resemble the U.S.–Singapore relationship, where the United States has no permanent base but enjoys access to Singapore's infrastructure and keeps a couple of hundred servicemen there to handle logistics. An arrangement with a slightly higher profile would be maintaining pre-positioned equipment and a "check-in facility" for possible U.S. reinforcements. A headquarters infrastructure without attached units might also be included in such an arrangement (as exists in Japan, where there is a U.S. Army corps headquarters but no combat soldiers). Some think that a small military advisory group would be the appropriate level of American military involvement in the region. Under these low-level-presence schemes, there could be rotating visits by U.S. forces to Korea for joint training and to signal continued U.S. commitment to Korea.

This solution would make it impossible for U.S. forces in Korea to do more than provide symbolic deterrence by their presence and would not enable the United States to take advantage of Korea's location in maintaining regional security. Rather than requiring the elevation of the Korea–U.S. strategic relationship to a higher plane, this solution would bring it to a lower level by removing most of the American forces. Continued joint deployment and training could, to some extent, maintain U.S.–ROK military ties, but not of the same magnitude as those that exist today.

A low-key U.S. presence would also remove some potential areas of conflict. The United States would not need to rely on Korean bases and facilities for regional contingencies and there would be far fewer American servicemen in Korea, thus diminishing the potential for tensions with the host nation.

The prevailing American opinion is that American military involvement in Korea should continue along the lines of the policy enunciated by the Pentagon in 1995 that "although United States ground forces will be needed for the foreseeable future ... the United States will continue to shift gradually from a leading to a supporting role within the coalition."[55] The Task Force on Managing Change on the Korean Peninsula of the Council on Foreign Relations advised that after unification the U.S. military presence in Asia should be "centered in Japan but include personnel on the

---

55. Department of Defense Office of International Security Affairs, *United States Security Strategy for the East Asia–Pacific Region*, Feb. 1995, p. 27.

Korean Peninsula"[56] to demonstrate American commitment to Korea, provide logistical support for U.S. forces in the western Pacific, and engage in joint training with ROK forces. Most of the individuals interviewed for this project believe that after unification the United States should tilt its presence in Korea toward having some air and naval presence and removing most U.S. Army units from the Peninsula. The U.S. Navy and Air Force would thus have the most important role in the American military structure in Northeast Asia.[57] These forces would deal with the security of sea lanes, prevent the spread of weapons of mass destruction, and maybe even fight international crime and drug trafficking. They would generate a sense of security in the region, but would not be there to fight a land war in Asia.

Under this scheme, most of the American army forces based in Korea, and perhaps some of the American ground forces located in Japan, would either be disbanded or moved to the United States, perhaps Alaska or the West Coast where they could be made more mobile, with an increase in transport aircraft and possibly some prepositioned equipment left in Asia, to enable them to return to the western Pacific in case of a crisis.

Such a decline in the U.S. military presence in Korea would loosen the ties between Washington and Seoul. The two countries would retain their formal alliance, but their military-to-military ties would be less extensive than they are today. There would be fewer areas of tension because there would be less need for the United States and Korea to cooperate in defense and security affairs.

As to American forces in Japan, the future of the marine forces in Okinawa will always be in jeopardy, especially if the marines lose some of their raison d'être after North Korea is removed from the scene. The rape of a young Okinawan girl by U.S. marines in 1995 and the killing of a Japanese civilian by a drunk marine in 1998 have continued to make the marine presence an issue that will not go away, despite the defeat of the anti-marine

---

56. Michael J. Green, project director, *Managing Change on the Korean Peninsula*, p. 40.

57. See Michael O'Hanlon, "Restructuring U.S. Forces and Bases in Japan," in Mike M. Mochizuki, ed., *Toward a True Alliance*, p. 150.

Ota Masahide in the November 1998 gubernatorial election. Part of the Okinawa base problem is an intra-Japanese dispute between Okinawans and Tokyo, but the fact remains that the large presence of so many U.S. servicemen on a small island will continue to be opposed by a significant section of the population and may one day become untenable. Moreover, to satisfy the Okinawans, the (already small) area available to U.S. forces was reduced from 249 km² in 1985 to 235 km² in 1998, and there will always be pressure for more cuts. This makes Okinawa less and less desirable because the ability of the marines to train is degraded every time the area available is reduced. As the threat perception declines after the demise of North Korea, it should be easier for opponents of the U.S. presence to convince fellow Okinawans and Japanese on the home islands that the marines should go. One idea has been to transfer them to Korea, where they could work jointly with the ROK Marines (Japan, unlike Korea, has no marine corps). They could rotate out of Korea for exercises overseas to lessen the social cost to Korea and could be located close to airports and seaports for mobility. This solution, however, would be difficult to implement. It would be expensive, and it is unclear who would pay for the new facilities the USMC would require on the Peninsula. Moreover, Koreans might feel that their country is used as a dumping ground for unwanted American servicemen from Japan.

In theory, it should be feasible to take advantage of Ground Self-Defense Forces (GSDF) facilities on the main Japanese islands to relocate the marines—or American soldiers—in other Japanese communities. In practice, the cost of such a move and the "not in my backyard" syndrome makes achieving such a transfer very complicated, unless a major crisis enables the governments to overcome these obstacles. Even if Americans used bases vacated by the GSDF, local opposition would arise because American military units generally require more space than most GSDF installations can provide, and have a training tempo that generates more noise and disturbance than that of the GSDF. Japan's high population density and mountainous terrain preclude finding any large unpopulated areas suitable for military bases and training grounds. Therefore, there is no location on the home islands where it would be possible to station an American division, or even a brigade, without disturbing some residents.

Finding a solution to the Okinawa problem is very important for U.S. strategy in the region. Even if the United States keeps a large and mobile army presence in Korea it would be risky for the United States to rely only on a Korea-based forward deployment in Asia. There is always a possibility that Korea might veto the use of Korean bases for American military actions that could harm Korea's relations with China or Russia. Though Korean-Chinese relations and China itself may develop in a way that is favorable to the United States, the geographic reality of Korea's situation means that the best China policy for Korea is sometimes at odds with American desires. This could also be the case for Russia, where America's policy is derived mostly from Russia's position as a European nation, whereas Korea's interest in Russia is focused on the Russian Far East. Consequently, it is important for the United States to have a base of operations in Japan in cases where American goals would be hampered by Korean policy.

Apart from the U.S. force structure in Asia, other issues will have to be addressed regardless of the number of American servicemen who remain in Asia. At this point, for instance, the senior U.S. general in Korea, a four-star U.S. Army officer, is simultaneously Commander of U.S. Forces Korea, UN Commander, and head of the Combined (ROK–U.S.) Forces Command (CFC), which has operational control over U.S. and Korean forces in wartime. Once the North Korean threat is removed, it may be impossible to keep an American in charge of this CFC if it is retained. Having a foreigner in operational control of the Korean army can be justified to the Korean public as an extraordinary measure made necessary by the North Korean menace. Once the Peninsula is pacified, however, it is unlikely that most Koreans will accept this state of affairs. (The NATO commander is still American. With 17 European members, it is easier to keep the top NATO job in U.S. hands; no matter who is in charge, at least 16 European states would have to accept a foreign commander, and some Europeans prefer an American to a European from another country.)

One alternative would be to organize U.S. forces in Korea along the same lines as those in Japan, that is, with an American commander in control of the Americans and the ROK government in control of the ROK forces, with no combined command. This solution, however, could weaken the ROK–U.S. bond and hurt the ability of the two countries to cooperate militarily, though ad hoc mechanisms could be devised to compensate for the dismantling of the CFC. Another solution, which would have the advantage of keeping the close Korean-American connection, would be to keep the CFC, or a new command with similar functions, but to put a Korean general in the top position, with an American deputy. That might lead to domestic U.S. opposition ("no Americans under foreign command") but it could be noted that from World War I to NATO there have been many cases of Americans serving under the operational control of foreign generals and admirals.

Regardless of the level of American deployment in post-unification Korea, in addition to the future of the command structure the United States will have to address the use of USFK units for out-of-Korea operations. At present, U.S. forces in Korea are tasked solely with the defense of South Korea against a possible Northern attack. After unification, the United States may wish to use its Korea-based forces elsewhere to deal with crises involving Taiwan, China, Russia, and Southeast Asia. This would require agreements with Korea regarding the use of Korean facilities for such operations. It would also probably necessitate ending the practice of having Korean soldiers (KATUSAs) serve in American units in Korea, because the ROK government is unlikely to let them serve overseas in American operations and there would be little use in having Koreans in U.S. Army units for deployment outside of Korea.

Therefore, the United States and the ROK will need to address the conditions under which the United States could use Korean military and civilian facilities in the case of contingencies involving U.S. forces in Korea in military activities outside of Korea. Such issues would include access to ports, airfields, railroads, hospitals, and priority use of transportation networks in an emergency; the provision of supplies and maintenance facilities; and military support (for example, search and rescue) by ROK forces for the United States. So far, the premise of Korean support for U.S. forces in Korea has been that the USFK would be fighting in Korea for the defense of the ROK and that obviously the ROK would provide all available support to the Americans. If the USFK assumes a regional role, the Korean government will want to revisit the terms and conditions under which U.S. forces operate in the country. Thus, regardless of the size of the post-unification USFK, it would benefit the United States and Korea to undergo a process similar to the Guideline Review for U.S.–Japanese cooperation to regulate the numerous issues associated with the possible use of American power from Korean bases.

The location of U.S. forces in Korea may also become an issue. The U.S. military occupies a large compound in downtown Seoul complete with a golf course. After unification, Koreans may wish to regain the use of this area for themselves, thus forcing the U.S. military to relocate.

The United States might also use the opportunity of the end of the Korean War to redesign its organizational command chart for Asia. Currently, the USFK is under a four-star army general. In his capacity as head of the USFK, he reports to Hawaii, where a four-star admiral is the Commander-in-Chief–Pacific (CINCPAC). But the same American general, as head of the CFC, is under the direct authority of the U.S. Secretary of Defense and the Korean Ministry of National Defense, and he also serves as head of the UN Command, though the United Nations does not have authority over American forces in Korea.

The organization of the U.S. armed services in Japan is complicated. The USFJ has a senior Air Force officer as commander, who is also Commander of the 5th Air Force, but the III MEF (Marine Expeditionary Force) in Okinawa is under the operational control of MARFORPAC (Fleet Marine Force Pacific) under CINCPAC. The 7th Fleet is based in Japan, but is not under the operational control of the USFJ. Moreover, American ground forces in Korea are army troops, but the U.S. ground presence in Japan is composed of marines, adding another difference between the USFK and the USFJ ground component.

Consequently, the United States might use this opportunity to alter its own military command architecture in the region to bring all its Northeast Asia forces under a single regional command, based in the region. Some analysts have suggested creating a U.S. Northeast Asia Command to bring all U.S. forces in Japan and Korea under the same command.[58] This would also provide

---

58. See, for example, Richard L. Bogusky, "The Impact of Korean Unification on Northeast Asia: American Security Challenges and Opportunities," *The Korea Journal of Defense Analysis* 10, no. 1 (summer 1998), p. 70.

the U.S. military with a senior-level point man for Northeast Asia, whereas today CINCPAC's theater is so large (from India to Hawaii) that he can only devote some of his energy to Northeast Asia. Others have argued that the possible gains from such a move would not outweigh the considerable costs of modifying current arrangements including the arduous interservice turf wars that always erupt when such changes occur.

Setting up a Northeast Asia Command would have strategic implications. It would not be possible for the United States to have its forces in either Japan or Korea under the operational control of headquarters located on one or the other side of the Tsushima Strait without much closer Japanese-Korean security ties. If a U.S. Northeast Asian Command is to have operational control over all American units in the two countries, it must be able to rely on cooperation between them. Both Japan and Korea would need to agree that American forces stationed on their soil could take part in operations in defense of the other country without any restrictions and, at a minimum, with some sort of rear-area support provided by Japan and the Republic of Korea. One idea would be to move 8th Army headquarters from Korea to Japan to command all U.S. Army forces based in Korea and Japan,[59] but that would require Japanese and Korean approval. Thus, a seemingly technical change can only be realized when there are strategic transformations. A Northeast Asia Command might, however, serve to speed such a transformation by gradually building a command infrastructure that would both require and facilitate Korean-Japanese cooperation.

TECHNOLOGY AND U.S. FORCES IN ASIA

BALLISTIC MISSILE DEFENSE

There are two technological developments that will affect U.S. forces in Northeast Asia. One is ballistic missile defense

---

59. See Robert Odell, *China, the United States, and Japan*, p. 42.

(BMD). Ballistic missiles will continue to proliferate in the coming decade, even if North Korea is defanged. Therefore, the momentum in favor of BMD will likely survive the collapse of North Korea. BMD could strengthen the interest of Japan and possibly Korea (though at this point it has not shown an interest in BMD) in further developing their military ties with the United States to take advantage of U.S. technology. This could be the basis of a strong U.S.-Korean-Japanese defense partnership, but it would depend on an American decision to proceed with BMD, allied desire to participate and to use U.S.–designed systems, and a willingness to confront Chinese and Russian opposition to BMD. Another challenge for the United States would be to integrate Taiwan into the umbrella without creating undue problems for Korean and Japanese ties with China.

REVOLUTION IN MILITARY AFFAIRS (RMA)

The second pivotal technological development is the revolution in military affairs (RMA, as it is known). The RMA concept, as understood by its most ardent supporters, is that new or emerging technologies will revolutionize warfare. Because of improved sensors and high-precision weaponry, combined with faster and more powerful microprocessors, air and space systems will defeat a technologically inferior foe with only a very limited input from ground forces. Therefore, as long as the United States retains a technological edge over its adversaries, it should be able to win any war it undertakes, thanks to the power of information processing and sophisticated machines. According to RMA enthusiasts, the United States defeated Iraq in 1991 owing to U.S. aerospace and computer assets, and the ground war was of secondary importance because the Iraqis had already been crushed by the time coalition tanks went into action against Iraqi positions. As the RMA gathers speed, the army will gradually lose its importance in warfare, and technology will remove the need for large numbers of soldiers in overseas postings, because aerospace and computer systems will kill any foe at hypersonic velocity or at the speed of light from orbital space, cyberspace, the upper atmosphere, the high seas, or the continental United States. "Scenario 2015: How Science Shapes War," published in *Jane's Defence Weekly* in

1997, describes a general with a staff of only four other officers who controls the entire U.S. operation (a hypothetical war in the Persian Gulf in 2015) from a command center, thanks to a "virtual retinal display, [where] auditory and motion cues have positioned her mind on a 'magic carpet' flying throughout the 3-D operational theatre."[60] This scenario, under which the United States achieves victory using aerospace, computer, and naval systems without the involvement of ground troops is a good, though extreme, example of some of the RMA concepts.

Not all believers in the RMA see it as revolutionary. Some think it is an evolutionary process but also believe that advanced aerospace weapons and information warfare will lessen the need to invest in infantry and armored units.

Other specialists take a radically different view of the evolution of warfare. They believe that technology actually favors land power. Advanced sensors make it more difficult for air and naval units to hide, because they stand out against the background of air or sea, but soldiers find it much easier to hide in the ground and are thus less vulnerable to advanced weaponry.[61] These scholars also cast doubt on the claims that Desert Storm demonstrated the superiority of air power. They note that American tanks destroyed more Iraqi tanks than the allied air forces, even though the terrain and the absence of an opposing air force facilitated the task of allied pilots.[62] Consequently, they consider that "America's next war, like those that have preceded it, almost certainly will be won—or lost—on land."[63] Accordingly, infantrymen and tanks will remain essential for American military power. They argue that "In pursuing our fascination with technology, we could weaken traditional alliances

---

60. Nick Cook et al., "Scenario 2015: How Science Shapes War," *Jane's Defence Weekly* (11 June 1997), pp. 58.

61. See Col. V. J. Warner, USA, "Technology Favors Future Land Forces," *Strategic Review* 26, no. 3 (Summer 1998), pp. 40–53.

62. See William E. Odom, "Transforming the Military," *Foreign Affairs* 76, no. 4 (1997).

63. LTG Paul Van Riper, USMC, and MG Robert Scales, USA, "Preparing for War in the 21st Century," *Strategic Review* 25, no. 3 (summer 1997), p. 15.

and deterrence as well as our support for the very values and political principles that make other countries respect and trust the United States."[64]

Apart from this technological debate, there is a *political* argument in favor of ground power. It is that the political goals of war can only be achieved through armies. "The object of warfare is to dominate a portion of the earth, with its peoples, for causes either just or unjust. It is not to destroy the land and people, unless you have gone wholly mad."[65] Air, space, and sea platforms help control the outcome of events on the ground and facilitate the task of the armies by providing information, destroying enemy targets, and transporting soldiers. But only physical occupation can allow a country to exert control over another nation. The United States managed to impose its will on (West) Germany in 1945 because Americans occupied the country, executed hostile officials or sent them into retirement, and dismantled the armed forces before reshaping them into a U.S.–friendly Bundeswehr. Because the United States did not occupy Iraq, its air and naval power were unable to topple Saddam Hussein.

If the RMA concept dominates American defense policy, it almost certainly will lead to a reduction in U.S. ground power in Asia and the rest of the world. First, the RMA supporters put less value on land power. Second, an "RMA force" consists of high-cost assets based in space, at sea, or in the United States rather than in foreign countries (B-2 bombers, for example). Third, the cost of equipping an RMA force would restrict the funding available for army and marine ground units. Those who do not believe in the RMA promise would spend less on new aerospace, naval, and computer devices and would devote more resources to land power, and thus more forces would be available for ground deployment in Asia. Consequently, the more successful the proponents of the RMA, the smaller U.S. ground forces in Asia will be. Air force units in Asia would also likely be re-

---

64. Michael O'Hanlon, "Can High Technology Bring U.S. Troops Home?" *Foreign Policy,* (Winter 1998–99), no. 113, p. 85.

65. T. R. Fehrenbach, quoted by Col. Harry G. Summers, Jr., (USA ret) in "The Korean War Paradigm," prepared for the Conference on "The Korean War: An Assessment of the Historical Record," 24–25 July 1995, p. 2.

duced in size because there would be less need for tactical air power and transport to support ground units.

FACTORS THAT WILL DETERMINE U.S. POST-UNIFICATION POLICY

Several factors and developments will help shape American policy after unification. The most important will be how the President and his national security team conceive America's role in Asia. This will depend on the unpredictable factor of who will be sitting in the Oval Office when Korea is unified. But other major factors will shape events.

U.S.–KOREAN RELATIONS

The state of U.S.–Korean relations will have a major impact on U.S. post-unification policy. If Americans perceive Korean policy as unfavorable to American interests, it is more likely that U.S. forces will not stay in the country after unification. Several issues in particular will be relevant to the perception of American-Korean relations in the United States.

The first is the level of Korean support for American goals in Asia. In particular, if Sino-American relations are bad and Korea is seen as not supportive of U.S. policy toward China, it will be more difficult to portray Korea as an ally of the United States in the post-unification period.

This could be a significant problem. Regardless of Korea's pro-American stance, it is logical for Seoul to have a policy toward China that is sometimes at odds with Washington's. The United States can choose to "engage" Beijing or it can decide to forget about China and sever all ties, as it did in the first decades of the Mao era. Korea, however, does not have the option to ignore its most powerful neighbor, and it has a far greater stake than the United States in avoiding confrontation with China (a comparison with Finland and the Soviet Union may be exaggerated but illustrates the point).

Japanese-Korean relations will also have some impact on whether Americans view Korea as an ally. If for any reason a united

Korea seems fairly hostile to Japan, it will be more difficult for the United States to maintain a strong security relationship with Korea. The more Japan and Korea are willing to cooperate with each other, the easier it will be for the United States to plan for a post-unification military posture in Asia.

The state of economic relations between Korea and the United States will also influence American policy. Korea's relations with the United States were damaged by the refusal, until the 1997 crisis, of the South Korean government to accept foreign investment and by Korea's anti-import mercantilist policy. Had Korea been open to foreign investment from the 1950s onward, American manufacturers would have set up subsidiaries in the ROK, both to sell to Koreans and to produce for export to third countries or back to the United States. In addition to improving the standard of living of Korean citizens, this would have enhanced Korean-American economic ties and given some American firms a stake in the Korean economy. A more liberal import regime would also have helped and deepened U.S.–Korea relations.

If Americans believe that Korea's post-crisis reforms have improved the climate for American business in Korea (which so far seems to be the case, though implementation is still an issue), it will improve Korea's standing in the United States. On the other hand, if Korea is seen as stonewalling on reform, it will hurt the prospect for strong Korean-American relations. Regardless of Korean economic policy, the national security arm of the executive branch (Pentagon, State Department) is likely to be "pro-Korean," but the attitude of Congress, the United States Trade Representative, and the Commerce Department and other economic agencies will be affected by the ROK economic and trade policy. American economic displeasure could also have an impact on ROK policy toward the United States if sanctions or aggressive trade-opening measures, to counter real or perceived Korean protectionism, lead to anti-Americanism in Korea.

A problem for Korea is that much of the trade friction may be caused by Korean exports and the opposition of protectionist lobbies in the United States, regardless of Korea's progress toward liberalizing trade. To some extent the liberalization of the ROK economy will make it easier for Korea to enlist support within the

United States and its business community, but this will not disarm protectionist forces.

U.S.–JAPAN RELATIONS

American-Japanese relations will also have a major impact on American post-unification policy in Asia. As in the case of Korean-American ties, there are both political and economic aspects of the relationship. On the political front, the more Japan is seen as "pro–United States" the better it will be for U.S.–Japanese relations. The new defense Guidelines, which demonstrate Japan's desire to contribute more to the Alliance, will have a positive effect (even if to some extent they only codify existing procedures and agreements). Attitudes toward China will also have an impact, though less than in the case of Sino-Korean relations; Japan, which does not share a border with China and is stronger than Korea, has less stake in good relations with Beijing, and thus it is easier to ensure that Japanese policy will be compatible with America's. It is also possible that at some point Japan may be more "hawkish" toward China than the United States, whereas unless Sino-Korean relations deteriorate enormously, Korea is likely to favor a "softer" attitude toward China.

Economic issues that affect U.S.–Japanese relations are fairly similar to those in Korea. Japan, like Korea, hurt U.S.–Japan ties (as well as its own people) by its opposition to foreign investment and imports. Investment practices have changed enormously, with Japanese firms, with the government's blessing, now seeking foreign buyers. The import regime has been liberalized, but many steps still need to be taken before liberalization is achieved. Decades were lost during Japan's "closed country" policies. But like Korea, Japan is often the victim of American protectionism, which has damaged U.S.–Japan relations. The state of the Japanese economy will also have an impact on U.S. perceptions. U.S.–Japan relations will be hurt if, as is now the case, American policymakers think that Japan is failing to revitalize its economy and thus is hampering world economic growth.

The better the relations among the United States, Japan, and Korea, the more likely less opposition will come from Congress and the public if the President decides to keep military forces in these nations. Good relations will not automatically lead to calls to maintain powerful USFK and USFJ forces, but bad relations will surely make it more difficult to justify an American military commitment to the defense of these two U.S. allies.

U.S.–CHINA RELATIONS

The state of Sino-American ties will affect American policy, but the way in which it will do so is not clear. If the relationship is peaceful, some Americans may argue that there is no need to keep American soldiers in Asia, because there is no threat (the problems of Korean-Japanese rivalry are rather unfamiliar to Americans, even to members of Congress). At the same time, if relations between Beijing and Washington are so good that China clearly favors the continued presence of American troops, it might make it easier for them to remain in Asia. If there are major tensions between China and the United States, there might be a push to keep U.S. forces in Asia to "contain" China. This would complicate Korean-American relations, unless Korean-Chinese relations also deteriorated abruptly and Korea wanted the USFK to protect the Peninsula from China. It is also possible that if Sino-American relations have deteriorated and Americans think that the United States is not powerful enough to deny China preeminence on the Asian mainland, the United States might decide to withdraw from Korea.

NEW THREATS

If Americans focus on the "new threats," such as terrorism, it will be more difficult for large U.S. forces to remain in Asia after Korean unification, because there will be calls to redeploy assets against terrorists or drug lords or to save failed states in the Third World. If these issues are deemed less important, however, it is more likely that U.S. forces will stay in Asia after unification.

CONGRESS AND ASIA

Relations between Asian states and Congress will also shape U.S. policy. Many diplomatic missions focus on the U.S. executive branch instead of making an effort to know and influence Congress, even though it is an important player in U.S. foreign policy. For foreign and military policy, the Congressional decision makers are the legislators who sit on the Armed Services and Foreign Relations Committees and some members of the Appropriations Committees, as well as their key staffers. These men and women are very influential and can force policies on an unwilling administration (for example, some of the sanction legislation against Cuba, which the Clinton administration does not favor) or prevent the president from implementing his own agenda (by obstructing trade agreements with China entry for example, or stopping fast-track legislation, passing the Taiwan Relations Act, vetoing arms sales, or blocking ambassadorial appointments). Even in cases where the president has won, as with NAFTA and Normal Trade Relations for China, the battles with Congress have forced the executive to compromise or back down on some other issues. Taiwan, cannot have formal relations with the executive branch because of America's derecognition in 1979, but has been highly effective in establishing close links with members of Congress from both sides of the aisle. As a result, Taiwan's interests are generally taken into account by Congress, which makes sure that the executive branch, generally more "pro-China," is more supportive of Taiwan than it would be otherwise. Japan and Korea have been less diligent in their congressional relations work, and if the governments of Japan and Korea want to maintain a strong American presence in Asia after unification, stronger ties with Congress will help them achieve their goals.

This may be particularly important for Korea with regard to its China policy. If Sino-American relations are tense, most members of Congress will expect America's allies to support American positions. If the Korean government wants to avoid jeopardizing its ties with the United States while simultaneously having a different China policy, it will profit by educating members of Congress and their staffs on Korea's rationale for following a different policy. Korea's China policy, unless it is radically divergent from America's, can be compatible with a strong U.S.–Korean military relationship. It will, however, require a major effort on Seoul's part to explain it.

DOMESTIC ISSUES

The fiscal climate in the United States, and the health of its economy, will also affect U.S.–Asian policy. The stronger the economy, the more probable it is that the declinist school will be overshadowed by those who think that America can afford to remain a military hegemon in Northeast Asia. The more the United States suffers from domestic problems or a sick economy, the less likely it is that Americans will be sufficiently optimistic to pursue an ambitious foreign policy and the more likely that they will be tempted to focus on issues closer to home.

If there is strong support for cutting government spending, lowering taxes, or increasing domestic social benefits, there will be a tendency to take advantage of the demise of North Korea and withdraw, or at least cut, U.S. military forces in Asia because slashing military spending is politically easier than reducing entitlements (for this to be achieved, however, forces brought to the United States would have to be disbanded, because they are not less costly in the United States than in Korea; in addition, new facilities would have to be built or old ones reactivated for them in America). Moreover, the economic strain of unification is likely to put an end to Korean Host Nation Support and other Korean contributions to the U.S. military in Korea. This could further erode support in the United States for the USFK, as the Host Nation Support argument has often been used to justify U.S. military deployment in Asia to Congress.

The state of the American military will also play an important role in post-unification policy. If the United States is still short of ground forces, some military planners may wish to deploy some of the soldiers now in Korea for use in other theaters or as a reserve force based in the United States. Members of Congress may hope that some of the U.S. units brought back to the United States and not disbanded could be located in their districts, where they would provide jobs and income for their constituents, and if U.S. forces are reduced, these congressmen may prefer that the cuts fall on overseas bases rather than on installations in their districts.

There are now a significant number of Korean-Americans, and proportionately far more among the most educated classes, but Korean-Americans as a group have had little impact on U.S.

policy in Asia. The Korean-born generation, often handicapped by cultural and language barriers, has not been very active in politics, and those born in the United States have successfully assimilated and are not particularly active in Korea-related activities. Moreover, Korean-Americans have not had any issue to rally around comparable, for example, to the desire of the Cuban exiles to overthrow Castro. In addition, unlike Cuban-Americans, who are concentrated in Miami, Korean-Americans are widely scattered across the United States, and the areas with the largest number of Korean-American voters, Los Angeles and New York City, are so big that the Korean-Americans are only one of the many immigrant groups, and not the largest one.

The business community will not have much of an impact on U.S. defense policy in Asia. American corporations benefit enormously from the U.S. military presence abroad. Without the U.S. military securing the peace in Asia and Europe, necessary for trade and investment, many American firms would become far less profitable or possibly even go bankrupt. Business, however, has not been very vocal in its support of a strong defense (except, obviously, for arms contractors). This situation is unlikely to change. It makes more sense for an economic actor to invest his energy in legislation that will benefit him almost exclusively and where his contribution to the lobbying effort plays a major role (say, for example, one of the few automotive manufacturers seeking profits through protectionism) than to expend his efforts on policies where his own input will have far less influence and where the outcome is likely to be the same whether he actually does anything or not. Moreover, few businessmen realize the importance of American military force in underpinning American prosperity.

BURDEN SHARING

Burden sharing may resurface as an issue in relations between the United States and its Asian allies. Some consider that with the world's second-largest economy (Japan) and two significant mid-sized economies (South Korea and Taiwan), America's Asian partners should take care of themselves. They find it shocking that Japan should spend so little, by U.S. standards, on defense. In addition, with the exception of a few soldiers in low-risk peacekeeping missions, Japan has never asked its servicemen to put their lives on the line for the common defense. Japanese mine-sweepers were dispatched to the Gulf but arrived after Iraq's defeat. According to this line of thought, the United States has spent a lot on guns, allowing Japan to produce a lot of butter, and by giving up its military leverage has allowed Japan and other Asian states to grow richer.

Burden sharing has been an issue in America's relations with Asia and Europe for decades, but as the perception of the threats decline, the issue is likely to become more important in the United States. The lower the threat perception, the more likely that Congress and voters will quibble over whether the allies are pulling their own weight

Japan has, however, made significant contributions to the U.S. alliance, including the largest financial contribution to the Gulf War, and hosts many American facilities on a crowded island. Korea has a large defense budget and subjects its young men to the draft. Moreover, supporters of continued American deployment do not look at burden sharing in the same light. They see the United States as providing a common public good and consider it normal for the United States, as the most powerful country, to contribute more than its share to the common defense.[66] Further, America's added military burden has not hurt the American economy, nor has it prevented Americans from enjoying a higher standard of living than Europeans and Japanese.

Moreover, the U.S. alliances with Asia and Europe benefit from the fact that the United States makes a disproportionate contribution to the common defense. This is due to both military and political factors. Militaries, even if they train together, are never able to operate jointly without some loss of performance. Armed forces have different levels of effectiveness and dissimilar doctrines, equipment, traditions, recruitment policies, educational systems, and procedures, not to mention different languages. Joint training and the development of standard operating procedures can mitigate some of these problems but cannot eliminate them completely.

---

66. For the theoretical underpinnings of this reasoning, see Mancur Olson and Richard Zeckhauser, "An Economic Theory of Alliances," *Review of Economics and Statistics* 48, no. 3 (August 1966).

With the United States providing most of the military force it is easier to create an effective military alliance, because (a) a large part of the coalition's contingent is American and thus is internally coherent, and (b) America's dominant position allows it to impose a unified set of procedures, usually its own, sparing American forces from experimenting with alien ones and avoiding endless debates with the smaller partners about creating a hybrid and untested system.

Politically, a coalition is only as strong as its weakest member because the opponent can target it—militarily, diplomatically, economically, politically—to break the united front. Napoleon did this during many of his campaigns, as did Germany when it took Russia out of the war in 1917 and the Allies when they forced Italy to switch sides in 1943. This does not mean that building coalitions is not an effective strategy, but the fact is that America's dominant role in the alliances allows it to keep the coalitions going and to deflect military or political attacks aimed at undermining them. Moreover, America's preponderant role in its alliances makes it possible to speed up the decision-making process, because the United States has overwhelming weight within the alliance (the Kosovo conflict of 1999 was somewhat different because the United States decided to eschew leadership and to settle on an air-only campaign.)

The 1991 Gulf War provides an illustration of this fact. During the Gulf War, the (non-Arab) ground forces' allied contingent was about 85 percent American, with a command structure composed almost exclusively of U.S. officers from the Central Command Headquarters, which relocated from Florida to Saudi Arabia for the war. If the Allies had sent forces based on a pro-rata allotment, instead of about 320,000 U.S. soldiers and marines assisted by a couple of European divisions, there would have been something like 130,000 U.S. soldiers and marines; 71,000 Japanese soldiers; and 6,000 South Koreans; along with 7,000 Australians from the southern hemisphere; and 36,000 Germans; 28,000 French; 24,000 British; 26,000 Italians; and smaller European contingents, such as 5,000 Belgians and 1,000 Portuguese; and 3,000 Turks and 3,000 Norwegians from non–EU European states. The naval and air forces would have been equally international, with air bases in the Gulf hosting pilots from as many different countries as an international airport. The coalition forces might have been commanded by an American with a Japanese deputy commander and a German chief of staff, and included a British admiral, a French air force general, and an American army general as component commanders, each supervising ships, aircraft, and tanks from many nations. This would have been burden sharing, but it would have been inefficient because it would have taken much more time for all these armies, navies, and air forces to learn how to fight together. Logistics would have been a nightmare. Devising battle plans would have been a herculean task, given the unequal capabilities of the forces engaged and their different doctrines. Controlling leaks would also have been far more difficult. Once the battle had started, the impact of different procedures and doctrines would have hurt the coalition. Allied servicemen would also have found it much harder to avoid fratricide, due to the greater difficulty in differentiating friend from foe caused by the great variety of electronic systems, vehicles, aircraft, and uniforms in the coalition's arsenal, in addition to language barriers.

The ability of General Schwartzkopf to run operations would have been hampered by the need to accommodate the desires of all partners. During the Gulf War, it was sufficient for President Bush to consult with some allies and then have the Pentagon issue orders to the theater commander. In a true burden-sharing coalition, it would have been necessary to establish a war council, chaired by the heads of state and governments of at least the major contributors, to argue about the instructions issued to General Schwartzkopf. The council would have had committees composed of foreign ministers, defense ministers, and chairmen of the joint staffs, and a permanent committee of special ambassadors, including military representatives, located in Ryad. Needless to say, such a structure would have been far less effective in defeating Iraq than the White House–Pentagon–Schwartzkopf chain of command.

In addition, Iraq could have sought special deals with some coalition members, thereby undermining its unity. For example, Saddam Hussein could have played on anti-American and anti-Turkish prejudices to sway Greece to withdraw its contingent, or on pacifist feelings in Japan and some European nations to get them to oppose their military involvement and force their governments to pull their troops from Arabia. Iraqi propaganda would have reminded Korean conscripts that they were fighting "under Japanese command." To compensate for this loss of efficiency, the allies might have had to send even more men to the Gulf, increasing costs and delaying Desert Storm/Saber, and perhaps forcing the United States to contribute as much as it did without "burden sharing" to make up for this Tower of Babel coalition. The result would at worst have been defeat, or at best a victory achieved with higher casualties and financial costs.

Some Americans will argue that it made sense for the United States to bear the burden to defend itself and its allies against the communists because the Cold War was an abnormal era requiring extraordinary measures to protect the Republic. But with the demise of the Marxist threat, they believe there are no threats that justify a large-scale U.S. defense effort. With regard to Korea, there will be the sentiment that the United States has fulfilled its original mission, that is, to stop, contain, and defeat communist imperialism. That mission having been accomplished, the forces should come home and the United States—along with Asia— should enjoy the peace dividend. This is the policy the United States followed after 1914 and (briefly) 1945, and in Europe after 1989, always with negative outcomes. As long as North Korea is around, the nefarious nature of the Pyongyang regime makes it difficult for those who oppose the American presence to win support in the United States. But once North Korea is history, those who oppose America's acting as a "world policeman" will be energized. They will also benefit from the fact that for the United States to stay in Korea would imply its having to reframe its commitment to Korea, thus opening a new line of debate.

How American policy is portrayed will also influence the outcome. If a continued deployment is "sold" as a long-term policy of keeping large American units in Asia, it may elicit a hostile reaction among Americans. The continued stationing of forces in Asia could, however, also be portrayed as a transitional measure, which to some extent it will be, though the transition could take 50 years or more. When NATO was created, it was not presented to the U.S. electorate as a mandate to keep hundreds of thousands of U.S. soldiers, sailors, and airmen in Europe for decades (partly because the government itself did not realize that the Atlantic Pact would lead to the permanent basing of large American armies, air forces, and fleets in Europe). Similarly, the decision to keep Americans in Korea can be explained as a temporary measure that will last as long as Korea deals with the aftermath of unification. In addition, the absence of an immediate direct threat may lessen opposition to the U.S. presence because few Americans will fear that the troops would be involved in a war. (It was easier to ratify NATO expansion in 1999 because few senators thought that there was a risk that Poland, the Czech Republic, and Hungary would require the activation of Article 5, which calls for the defense of allies under attack, on their behalf.)

Moreover, if the United States is to stay in Japan and Korea, it will be essential that the issue also be framed in ideological or ethical terms. As Seymour Martin Lipset notes, it is important to portray U.S. foreign policy aims as righteous.[67] The unification of Korea, if the U.S. President wants to maintain an active U.S. military involvement in the region, should be presented as a triumph for American ideals, which it will be. The continued commitment to Korea would thus be shown to be part of America's desire to strengthen democracy in a country whose northern half has just been freed from communism. The horror stories that will be revealed to the world following the breakdown of communism should also help convince Americans of the moral aspect of the intra-Korean conflict and of America's duty to help a reunified Korea.

The question of the magnitude of America's post-unification military deployment in Northeast Asia will not be one that divides politicians across a predictable left/right or Republican/Democrat divide. Rather, opposition will come from several quarters, including the following:

- Politicians who think that money should be spent on domestic programs rather than on defense;
- Maybe trade unions who oppose Asia as a competitor, an interesting shift because during the Cold War most of the mainstream union movement was strongly anticommunist and committed to America's international role;
- Extreme fiscal conservatives who oppose government spending for almost anything;

---

67. Seymour Martin Lipset, *American Exceptionalism*, pp. 63–64.

- "America First" reactionaries, like Pat Buchanan, who sometimes favor unilateral American military action but oppose
long-term commitments to allies; and
- Those, as noted earlier, who think that the focus of America's
defense policy should move away from large conventional
forces to units tailored to fight piracy, crime, drugs, terrorism,
and other "post–Cold War" threats.

Support for a strong presence will come not only from the
traditional supporters of a strong "internationalist" security posture,
but also from general inertia. There is always a tendency to avoid
change. In particular, if American forces were removed from East
Asia, there is a possibility that they would be disbanded rather than
relocated. Thus, the armed services, in particular, will have an incentive in seeking to maintain the status quo.

IF THE PRC DISAPPEARS BEFORE THE DPRK

Most analysts assume that the basic political systems of the
major players around Korea will not change. This is accurate for
the United States and Japan. Barring some cataclysmic development, they will remain rich liberal democracies. China's fate, however, is much more difficult to predict. There are many reasons to
believe that the communist regime will not last another 20 years,
but divining the shape of a post–communist state is not possible.
(Russia's future is uncertain, but Russia is relatively peripheral to
the Korean question and will probably remain so.)

There are several major obstacles to continued communist
rule. Having jettisoned ideological purity, the party relies on delivering a rising standard of living to legitimize its rule. However,
China's rate of growth has declined because of the 1997 Asian
crisis, the political and social obstacles to further market-oriented
reform, the financial burden caused by the state-owned enterprises,
and the weakness of the legal system. This brings into question
the regime's legitimacy.

To control China's metamorphosis, the ruling party needs
to change while remaining strong and disciplined until other ways
are found to run the country. Unfortunately for the party, it has
decayed rather than developed. It has abandoned some of its tools
of social control. With the dismantlement of the planned economy,

the party's primary organizations at the work unit level have lost their ability to control their members.[68] But the party has not developed alternative ways of ruling the country or attempted to develop an "outside of the party" movement, such as the one that occurred in Taiwan in the waning years of the KMT's monopoly.

Moreover, increased personal freedom, which is required for economic growth, is a danger for the regime. It is far easier to maintain political stability in a harsh totalitarian state, than in China. In today's China there is a modicum of personal freedom, somewhat comparable to the Latin American autocracies of the 1960s and 1970s. These systems are often the least stable. Totalitarian tyrannies rule with an iron fist, and the only danger to the rulers comes from their colleagues within their own small ruling circle or from the armed forces. Bourgeois democracies may often change governments (about once a year in Italy since 1945), but the society is stable and there are rarely revolutionary policy changes. Countries like China, however, do not have the means to properly institutionalize and channel social mobilization and satisfy rising expectations, and they lack the means to repress these demands effectively. Contacts with the outside world, which have expanded greatly in China since the 1970s, weaken the regime by allowing foreign influences to corrupt the people and agitators and dissidents based abroad can stay in touch with the local population. Stability is thus more difficult to maintain. China must also deal with the risk of intra-elite disputes degenerating into organized violence. Therefore, "soft" dictatorships like Jiang Zemin's are less secure than Mao's murderous republic.

Finally, if the center weakens, China always faces the risk of disturbances in its periphery (Tibet, Xinjiang, maybe Inner Mongolia, and, in different ways, Hong Kong). The non-Han may be less than 10 percent of the population, but they occupy large territories and are located in border regions, which facilitates secessionist agitation. Even within the Han core of the country, regionalism remains strong and a few feeble centers can easily lead

---

68. Feng Chen, "Rebuilding the Party's Normative Authority: China's Socialist Spiritual Civilization Campaign," *Problems of Post-Communism* 45, no. 6 (Nov.-Dec. 1998), p. 40.

to some provinces breaking away from Beijing's control, or at least undermining central government authority.

Therefore, in five or ten years the Communist Party may lose power. But it is unclear what could succeed it. Unlike its sister organization on Taiwan (the KMT), the Communist Party has not created the basis for a solid bourgeoisie that could lead a liberal transition. There is no significant property-owning private sectors in middle-class China. Though Maoism is a thing of the past, the rule of law has yet to be established. The legal system is underdeveloped and it takes decades, at best, to develop one. This is a major difference between China and Chile, Argentina, or Spain, all of which had a much more advanced and liberal system of property rights under their dictators than China has had under any regime.

The examples of other post-communist states point to an unpleasant mix of illiberalism, economic disappointment, and social and political upheavals. The few post-communist societies that have escaped such failures are some Central European and Baltic nations, which have the advantage of proximity to the West, small populations, and stronger pre-communist foundations than China, including rule of law, civil society, and a cadre of educated men and women rooted in the Western tradition of these states.

Optimists might hope for a better outcome for China. China has benefited from almost a quarter-century of growing intercourse with the free world. Many Chinese have studied in free countries and have returned to China. Contacts with Hong Kong, Taiwan, Singapore, and Chinese immigrants in the West have exposed many Chinese to the achievements of Chinese who live under rule-of-law regimes. One might even imagine that the KMT, whose success in transforming itself from the tool of a dictatorship into the leading party of a prosperous democracy, could regain a foothold on the mainland and bring its political know-how to China.

What would be the implications of a new Chinese regime on America's Asia policy? Much would depend on the nature of the new China. A non-communist Chinese state could be an aggressive nationalistic country, a relatively peaceful post-communist state, a nation in civil war, or more than one country if some regions broke up from the center. It could be fairly prosperous or very poor.

If the Communist Party loses power in China, the United States will support liberal elements there. This could entail overt and covert support to political groups within China. It could also involve U.S. assistance in setting up a system of property rights and law courts.

But the United States, Taiwan, Japan, and other liberal democracies would have to be very modest in assessing their influence and its chances of success. China has more than 1.2 billion people and has very little in common with the developed democracies. Even Taiwan is very different, having been under a separate administration for 101 of the past 105 years. The vast majority of Chinese have never been abroad nor met a foreigner. China's future political course will depend on what the Chinese do, not on American actions.

Therefore, the United States will have to avoid excessive optimism and realize that its Northeast Asian alliances with Japan and Korea are the key to its Asian policy. Efforts to prematurely include a half-reformed China into the U.S.–Japanese–ROK triangle would only dilute the American alliance systems. Obviously, if a new Chinese regime is collaborative, the United States and its allies could offer it symbolic rewards, such as participation in summit meetings or inclusion in some sort of Organization for Security and Cooperation in Europe (OSCE)–type organization for East Asia and a Partnership for Peace–like program to establish military-to-military ties. But for the foreseeable future, China will stay outside the U.S. – Japan – Korea core and is likely to remain unpredictable.

The PRC "threat" is not the main reason for a continued American presence in East Asia. The American military deployment cements the U.S.–Japan and U.S.–Korean alliances and has a beneficial impact on Korean-Japanese relations. These reasons will remain valid regardless of developments in China.

For those who oppose continued American deployment in Asia, the overthrow of the current regime would strengthen their case. They would argue that with the end of Asian communism (although Vietnam might remain communist, but it is decrepit and far from Northeast Asia) there is no justification left for American power in Asia. They would also argue that an American military presence would provoke the new Chinese regime and weaken pro-American elements. The same arguments were made about NATO after the collapse of the Soviet Union and are likely to be made in the Asian context if and when Chinese communism breaks down.

However, if China does become noncommunist and relatively friendly to the United States, there will be one very favorable outcome: it will solve Korea's dilemma of having to balance strong military ties with the United States with good relations with China. This would significantly facilitate the management of ROK–U.S. security relations.

CONCLUSION

Before World War II, American strategy, regardless of how well-intentioned it was, did not give the United States the influence necessary to prevent war. The United States did not possess enough military power and lacked reliable allies in Asia. Even a nation as powerful as the United States cannot be a power in Asia without Asian partners. Geography, economics, and demography allow the United States to unilaterally dominate the Caribbean littoral. Northeast Asia is too far, too rich, and too large (in size and population) for the United States to achieve regional hegemony on its own. Japan, with the region's largest economy, a stable government, and a good location, is the indispensable partner of the United States in Asia. All the multilateral agreements and conferences of American interwar diplomacy were no substitute for U.S. military power and a Japanese alliance.

China is currently hostile to the United States, and even if it were not it is too poor and unstable to be a viable partner. Korea can play an important role, but by itself it is not strong enough to provide an anchor for the United States in Asia. Its economy is too small and it is cut off from the United States by a chain of Japanese islands, thus requiring a pro-American Japan to be a useful U.S. ally. But once Japan is established as the anchor of American defense policy in Asia, it will be vital for the United States to include Korea in its alliance structure for several reasons.

First, Korea is increasingly important in its own right, with a medium-sized economy and a post-unification population of 65 million people. American security is considerably enhanced by ensuring that the U.S. alliance has a monopoly on technologically advanced nations, because if developed countries are in the American sphere, this denies their economic and technological resources to potential enemies.

Second, as noted earlier, Korea matters to Japan. A Korea that is outside the American orbit is potentially threatening to Japan. Thus, a U.S.–Korea military alliance is one of the major American contributions to Japanese security. If the United States failed to maintain Korea in the U.S. sphere, it would fail to keep its side of the bargain with Japan.

Third, with no American troops in Korea, Japan would be the only Asian state hosting American forces. This could fuel opposition from some Japanese, who might fear their country would be "singled out" as the only nation in the region with American servicemen on its soil.

Moreover, U.S. forces must be forward-based in Asia. It is not possible to keep forces in the United States and deploy them in an emergency. Even with modern technology, the "tyranny of distance" is still a fact of life, and Hawaii is as far away from Korea as New York City is from Moscow. Forces stationed in Hawaii, Alaska, or California are too far from Asia, not only in travel time but also in terms of understanding the theater in which they would operate. It is difficult to have a "feel" for Korea when one is playing golf in tropical weather while Korea is covered with winter snows. In addition, having forces in Japan allows the United States to respond to potential crises by simply heightening their state of alert. Without forces there, moving men and materiel to Asia could itself be very difficult because it could be opposed by those who would see it as a dangerous escalation (and a big expense). Thus, the ability of the United States to maintain stability in the region would decline because military power is the key to America's ability to promote peace in the region.

The history of international relations in East Asia strengthens the argument for continuing a strong U.S. military presence in the region, anchored on alliances with Japan and Korea.

One cannot speak of "international relations" in Northeast Asia before the 19th century, because instead of a community of states there existed only the Middle Kingdom, with a small state (Korea), a remote island empire (Japan), and various groups of tribesmen. Russian expansion brought the Russian Empire into direct contact with China. Other Europeans also got involved in the region from the sea. But Japan's seclusion, which was nearly total after the enforcement of the sakoku (closed country) policy in 1638, meant that one of the major countries in the region was absent from the diplomatic game. Moreover, the slow rate of communications further isolated Northeast Asia from the rest of the world.

The European push into East Asia, combined with America's thrust into the Pacific, brought Northeast Asia into world politics. It also marked the first globalization of international affairs from a Northeast Asian point of view because Japan became a major player in international relations.

Thus, by the time the Anglo-Japanese alliance was signed in 1902, several powerful nations had worldwide military interests, and events in one part of the world affected the balance of power around the globe (the pre–19th century European empires never extended to Northeast Asia, except for Siberia). The imperial ambitions of the industrial states combined with the telegraph and the steamship to transform the world into a single strategic space operating in near-real time.

In Northeast Asia, the period from the Opium War to the Russo-Japanese War (1840–1905) was violent. The Europeans attacked China; Japan, itself subjected to unequal European treaties, fought China and Russia and occupied Korea. The United States conquered Spanish possessions, and the Europeans, Japanese, and Americans joined forces to invade Beijing in the wake of the Boxer Uprising. But from the Japanese victory against Russia in 1905 to the invasion of Manchuria in 1931, there were no major international wars in Northeast Asia (there was Japanese-Bolshevik fighting in Siberia, with American participation, but it did not degenerate into a full-fledged conflict). There were frequent uprisings and rebellions in China, but no wars that drew in the great powers.

Thus, the 1905–31 period was the only era of peace prior to 1953, but it was fragile and unstable. Peace in the region, after 1905 and before 1914, was ensured by a balance of power anchored on the Anglo-Japanese Alliance. The United States accepted the situation, and anyhow it could not challenge the established order because it lacked the military means to enforce its will in the region. China was impotent but it survived, albeit only as a semicolonized state. Korea and Taiwan were under firm Japanese control.

The post–Russo-Japanese War equilibrium broke down almost as soon as it came into existence. The U.S. government, initially unconcerned with Japan's metamorphosis into a modern imperialist state, was dissatisfied with Japanese exclusion of U.S. business interests in Manchuria after 1905. For its part, Tokyo feared U.S. ambitions in the Pacific following America's conquest of the Philippines and Guam.[69] Moreover, Japan did not favor the American Open Door policy for China.[70] For the United States, which had powerful corporations but no military strength in China, an open door regime was desirable because it would allow American firms to compete on an equal basis with foreign enterprises and, thanks to the strength of American business, to thrive. But for Japan, whose economy was small (its 1914 GDP was only 5.4 percent of that of the United States), the Open Door looked like a bad idea. The Japanese private sector was weaker than America's, and to Japan's mercantilist government it seemed more advantageous to divide China into semi-exclusive zones. In that way, Japanese power could enforce favorable treatment for Japanese conglomerates in areas of China under Japanese influence. Finally, racial animosity in the United States against the Japanese further contributed to damaging Japanese-American ties.

American concerns about Japanese intentions resulted in America's planning for war against Japan (War Plan Orange) in 1906. Until 1914, however, latent tensions between Japan and the United States were not very destabilizing because America was

---

69. Ian Nish, "Japan's Policies Toward Britain," in James W. Morley, ed., *Japan's Foreign Policy,* p. 203–204. Hosoya Chihiro, "Japan's Policies Toward Russia," in James W. Morley, ed., *Japan's Foreign Policy,* p. 376.

70. Walter LaFeber, *The Clash*, p. 75.

a marginal military player and the Anglo-Japanese alliance formed the backbone of the diplomatic system in Asia. But Britain's strength was crippled by World War I. The United Kingdom's power relative to Japan in East Asia declined drastically, changing this essential parameter of the balance-of-power equation. The United Kingdom could not provide security for Japan against Soviet Russia or its other foes, and Japan could free itself from its dependence on the Royal Navy. European holdings in Northeast Asia were at the mercy of Japan's army and navy after 1918. In addition, the Russian Empire was replaced by the Bolshevik state, whose ideology was committed to the destruction of noncommunist polities. As such, Soviet Russia did not play according to the established rules of diplomatic behavior and fomented revolutionary movements in China while attempting to do so in Korea and Japan.

Finally, as Chinese nationalism gained strength, it became increasingly difficult to treat China as a passive pawn. The rise of a militant Chinese nationalist movement complicated relations between the powers. The United States had relatively little to lose from Chinese nationalism, and many Americans supported the Chinese for strategic or sentimental reasons, whereas Japan feared the consequences of Chinese assertiveness on its holdings in China. A strong China jeopardized Japan's influence there and could deprive Japanese businesses of the Chinese market. China might also align with other adversaries of Japan and in the longterm, challenge Japanese control over Korea. The governments of Britain and France also disliked the rise of a stronger China, which would undermine their informal empire in China and their colonies in Southeast Asia. But London and Paris could not work in tandem with Tokyo because of the fear that Japan would sooner or later seek to expel Europeans from Asia to establish Japanese hegemony, and of the need of the West Europeans not to deviate too much from U.S. policy.

In addition, following the Great War, taking advantage of London's weakened position, the United States pressured Britain to sever the Anglo-Japanese alliance.[71] Instead, Washington created a "new concert of power" to replace the imperialistic equilib-

---

71. Akira Iriye, *The Globalizing of America*, p. 76.

rium.[72] The United States tried to limit naval armaments (at the Washington Conference and later the London Conference) and to foster stability through the Four Power Pact on regional security (United States, United Kingdom, France, Japan), the Nine Power Agreement on cooperation over China, and the Kellogg-Briand Pact outlawing war.[73]

These multilateral accords and disarmament initiatives failed. Japan's military ties to the West (the British alliance) were ruptured, and Japan was further alienated by Western racism (refusal of a clause of racial equality at Versailles and the 1924 U.S. Asian Exclusion Act).[74] If the United States had replaced Britain as Japan's partner in Asia or teamed with Britain to create a U.S.–Japan–UK alliance, and had increased its military power in the region, an American-Japanese alliance might have replaced the Anglo-Japanese one as the core of the Asian security system. Such a policy, however, would probably have failed, due to the impact of Chinese nationalism and of conflicting Japanese and American ambitions in Asia. This option was not tried and Japan, cast adrift without allies, felt threatened by Western hostility, Chinese nationalists abroad, and Marxism and other forms of subversion at home. Moreover, its fragile experiment with a constitutional government, which had never provided a liberal parliamentary monarchy, collapsed, and extremists brought about a more aggressive Japanese policy in Asia.

The first major overt challenge to Northeast Asian peace was the 1931 Japanese invasion of Manchuria. The Western powers and China were either unable or unwilling to respond to this development, and their lack of action explains why they failed to deter Japan from invading China proper following the 1937 "Marco Polo Bridge Incident." Ultimately, the war spread to Southeast Asia and the Pacific as Japan's leaders became more and more expansionist, and the United States decided it could not accept Japanese hegemony over the Greater East Asia Co-Prosperity Sphere.

---

72. Akira Iriye, *The Cold War in Asia*, p. 17.

73. See Akira Iriye, *The Globalizing of America*, pp. 82–83.

74. Alexander DeConde, *A History of American Foreign Policy*, third edition, vol. 2: *Global Power*, p. 104.

The United States limited its opposition to Japanese expansion to diplomatic measures ("nonrecognition" of Japan's occupation of Manchuria) and, in the last year prior to Pearl Harbor, to economic sanctions. This failed to stop Japan because the United States was militarily marginal in Asia. American aid to China had a negligible effect, and the American position in the Philippines remained at the mercy of a Japanese attack. Neville Chamberlain's contemptuous statement in 1937 that "It is always best and safest to count on nothing from the Americans but words"[75] was an apt description of U.S. policy. A decade earlier in 1927, Yoshida Shigeru, had already noted accurately that "its agreement [speaking of the United States] or disagreement should not be of great concern."[76] Neither Chamberlain nor Yoshida would have thought along those lines if the United States had been Asia's strongest military power. As Akira Iriye noted, referring to Asia earlier in the century, "the United States was trying to play the role of an Asian power without military power"[77] and failed. The United States had the world's largest navy but only a very small army and absolutely no allies of any significance in the region. Given America's posture in Asia, its reliance on words and treaties instead of actions and effective diplomacy backed by force, it is understandable that Japanese generals and admirals failed to take the United States seriously. Even by 1936, when it was clear that the world situation was explosive, the United States had fewer ground forces than Japan (183,000 vs. 256,000)[78] and except for fewer than 12,000 soldiers in the Philippines, there was no major American military presence west of Hawaii. In addition, unlike Japan, the United States did not have conscription.

As for Britain, it was too weak to counter Japan, and its fear of Chinese nationalism, which was directed against Britain as well as Japan, further limited London's options for stopping Japanese inroads on the mainland. China, poor, weak, and in the throes of a civil war, was no match for Japan's military machine. Thus, this

---

75. Akira Iriye, *The Globalizing of America*, p. 157.

76. John W. Dower, *Empire and Aftermath*, p. 74.

77. Akira Iriye, *The Cold War in Asia*, p. 35.

78. *Statesman's Year-Book 1937*, figures rounded to the nearest thousand.

precarious balance of power failed to contain the crises resulting from Japanese expansionism, Chinese militancy, British weakness, Soviet bolshevism, and American inconsistency, and from 1931 onward the war in Asia expanded until, by August 1945, every nation or faction capable of waging war was involved in the conflict.

The breakdown of Asia's equilibrium led to many years of fighting and tens of millions of fatalities (almost all Asian). After 1945, the Northeast Asian balance of power was totally altered. Japan was defeated and Britain was no longer a significant regional actor. Mao's forces gained the upper hand in the civil war, the Soviet Union had established a communist regime in North Korea, and South Korea became independent, though economically weak and politically fragile.

The United States maintained a military presence in Japan during the occupation (1945–1952) and thereafter with the ratification of the United States–Japan Security Treaty. This made it clear the United States wanted to keep Japan in its camp and would fight for it if needed.

In Korea, however, the United States went into retrenchment in the immediate postwar years. It had withdrawn all of its forces from South Korea in 1949, save for a Military Assistance Group. The United States stated its commitment to the Republic of Korea[79] but did not keep combat forces on the Peninsula.[80] This lack of concrete American commitment on the ground explains the Chinese Communist belief, reportedly stated by Mao Zedong, that "the Americans will not enter a third world war for such a small territory."[81] Only after three years of bloody fighting, millions of Koreans dead, wounded, or displaced, and tens of thousands of American fatalities, did the United States decide to maintain permanent military forces on the Korean Peninsula.

The pattern of communist behavior in the first decade of the Cold War was to expand their realm but to avoid a confronta-

---

79. Chen Jian, *China's Road to the Korean War*, p. 120.

80. William Stueck, *The Korean War*, p. 35.

81. Kathryn Weathersby, "New Russian Documents on the Korean War," in Woodrow Wilson International Center for Scholars, Cold War History Project, *Bulletin* no. 6–7, p. 31.

tion with the U.S. military, even in places like Berlin where the local correlation of forces was in their favor. Therefore, it is unlikely that the North Koreans would have launched an invasion in 1950 if there had been an American armored corps in Korea, backed by tactical air power. Moreover, even if North Korea had attacked, a strong and well-trained U.S. military force in South Korea would have repelled the North Korean People's Army promptly and at a much lower cost in blood and money.

Since 1953, when the Korean War armistice was signed and Japan regained its sovereignty, Northeast Asia has been at peace. The Beijing and Pyongyang regimes slaughtered millions of Chinese and North Koreans, but for Asians inside the U.S. defense perimeter, save for a few incidents along the DMZ and around Taiwan's outlying islands, there has been uninterrupted peace since 1953.

The post-1953 era is the first truly stable period of international peace for Northeast Asia since the mid–19th century when Western invasions, nationalism, and industrialization transformed Asia. Before 1914, peace depended on a fragile balance of power that needed to be finely tuned among several nations. The peaceful status quo failed to survive the consequences of World War I, but it would probably not have lasted for much longer, even absent the European conflagration and the rise of bolshevism. It could not successfully adapt to declining British power, rising Japanese strength and ambitions, growing American sympathy for China and American imperial interest in the Pacific, and Chinese nationalism. World War I merely precipitated the decline of a system inherently prone to war. In some ways, the countdown to the next war started with the signing of the Portsmouth Treaty that ended the Russo-Japanese War. The current architecture is far more stable because it is based on overwhelming U.S. power and unconditional U.S. alliances with Japan and Korea anchored in a strong military commitment.

The post-1953 system is different in several ways from the previous international regimes that existed in Northeast Asia.

First, a permanent military presence of the United States in the region makes it impossible to doubt that the United States would fight for Korea or Japan. Moreover, the physical presence of American troops has considerably reinforced the effectiveness of American alliances in Asia. For both Korea and Japan, the deployment of U.S. forces on their territories has allowed their militaries to forge links with the American military through joint training, the shared use of facilities, and mutual military planning. This enhances both the potential combat effectiveness of U.S. forces in Asia and each country's own ability to fight and win a war in conjunction with its Asian allies.

As a result of these close U.S.–ROK and U.S.–Japan interactions, members of the Korean and Japanese military have some familiarity with their American counterparts. Given the great cultural differences between Asia and the United States, this military-to-military relationship has been one of the most important human links between the United States and its Asian allies.

These military relations have also had a profound impact on the U.S. military. Though not all U.S. officers have served in Korea and Japan, many have spent time in these countries. Today most of the senior generals and admirals of the U.S. armed services have been posted at least once in Korea or Japan, and all of the top officers of the U.S. services travel to Asia from time to time for talks with allies and to inspect American units stationed there. When the United States divided Korea for the purpose of accepting the surrender of Japanese forces in 1945, few Americans knew anything about Korea, and Washington made decisions without consideration for Korean interests and pride. The state of knowledge about Japan was better, but still far from adequate. After half a century of close U.S.–Korean relations, the picture is vastly different. The United States now has a reservoir of senior military officials familiar with Korea and Japan who have served there and worked with their Asian counterparts, and there are even a few specialists who have attended Japanese and Korean military schools. In Korea, U.S. personnel serve on the same staffs and in some cases, in the same units as Koreans. The participation of Japanese and Korean officers in U.S. military or civilian education programs and officers stationed in the United States for liaison or procurement work has also strengthened the ties between the militaries of the United States and its Asian allies.

It is not possible to quantify the impact of the personal connections that have been developed due to the U.S. forward deployment in Korea and Japan. These connections have not prevented misunderstandings or disputes. They have, nevertheless, greatly facilitated the management of U.S. relations with Japan and Korea. American military and civilian officials with a good knowledge of Northeast Asia can inform senior policy-makers and also maintain close contact with their Asian counterparts, thanks to the networks of colleagues they have developed in Asia. These interactions have also ensured that the alliances would work better in case of war, and have therefore strengthened their credibility. An alliance that consists only of a few treaties requires time to be transformed into a mechanism that makes joint military action possible; it is therefore less potent and has less deterrence power. During the Gulf War of 1990–91, for example, the British found it easier to operate within the U.S.–led coalition than the French did. Both Britain and France are signatories of the Atlantic Alliance, only Britain is part of the integrated NATO structure. Thanks to immigration and business, cultural, and educational exchanges, other bonds have since developed between the United States and its Northeast Asian allies. The military-to-military ties, however, remain essential because they connect senior government officials on opposite sides of the Pacific and have a direct impact on the fighting capability of the allies.

Second, the American presence has also had a formidable impact on domestic political developments. In Japan, the present constitution (technically an amendment to the 1889 charter), which provided Japan with its first real experience of liberal democracy, was written by an American lawyer on the occupation staff. The continued U.S. presence after 1953, when the occupation ended, strengthened liberal democracy. This has been particularly important because prewar Japan, notwithstanding the Taisho Democracy years, never had a functioning liberal democratic regime; the armed forces had escaped parliamentary control, and the definition of lèse-majesté was extremely broad. Many politicians who ran Japan after the war were holdovers from the pre-1945 era who cared little about freedom and democracy, but the U.S. link ensured that these postwar leaders would not return Japan to autocracy because they wanted continued American support for Japan more than they longed for a return to prewar authoritarianism.

In South Korea the United States tolerated autocratic governments, and many Koreans blamed the U.S. military for having facilitated General Chun Doo Wan's coup d'état in 1980. Nevertheless, the enhanced protection provided by the USFK probably helped Koreans feel that they were secure enough from attack and could therefore risk democratization in the 1980s. The U.S. link also makes it far more difficult for Korea to backslide away from democracy because of the crisis this would engender in Korean–U.S. relations.

Third, thanks to the economic growth of Japan and Korea since the 1950s, which would have been impossible without a stable international order, economic ties between Northeast Asia and North America (and Europe) have led to the development of economic and business ties that did not exist before World War II. There have been many episodes of transpacific trade friction, but trade between the United States and Japan and Korea, along with the large Japanese foreign investment in the United States, has added a new dimension to Northeast Asia's ties to the United States. Thus, apart from being enmeshed in a strong and resilient military alliance with the United States, Japan has been integrated into the world economy. Through forums such as the G7 and the frequent meetings between American and Japanese economic policy-makers, the country now plays a role in international economic and financial decisions.

The forces that undermined peace prior to 1945, that is, nationalism, regional rivalries, and political instability, are still present in Asia in 2000 and could easily regain their potency without the influence of U.S. power. Without the U.S. military presence and the U.S.–Japan–Korea alliance, Northeast Asia would return to a situation of great- and small-power rivalries that would undermine regional peace.

PLANNING FOR THE FUTURE

This study has argued that the United States must remain the strongest military power in Northeast Asia and continue to anchor its Asia policy on the Japanese-American and U.S.–Korean alliances.

Despite the concerns caused by the North Korean nuclear and missile program, there has actually been relatively little change in Northeast Asia in the past few years. The ROK–U.S. forces can deter a North Korean attack, and war is unlikely. Recent changes in U.S., Japanese, and South Korean policies have been gradual. Japan and the United States have developed a new set of guidelines, and the ROK and Japan have started to increase their cooperation in the security field. These developments are positive, but they are rather timid, and more ambitious initiatives are needed.

Looking to the future, what concrete steps can the United States, Japan, and Korea take to strengthen regional security?

The first step would be to continue improving Korean-Japanese security ties. The healthier the Korean-Japanese relationship, the easier it will be to manage the transition from a divided to a unified Korea. Peacekeeping missions could provide the justification for the development of ROK–Japan security ties. Korea and Japan, perhaps in coordination with the United States, could jointly participate in peacekeeping operations (PKOs). This would provide an opportunity for Korean and Japanese servicemen to work together. This cooperation is likely to come about slowly, but that will avoid provoking segments of public opinions that are not yet ready for such developments. However, the long lead time is a reason to move it forward sooner rather than later. Especially important, in the context of Japanese-Korean relations, Tokyo and Seoul will have to develop an understanding of some post-unification issues such as the fate of the North Korean nuclear program and their continued adherence to a policy of not acquiring nuclear weapons.

Peacekeeping is also one area that should be developed to strengthen American support for the U.S. presence in Asia. As explained earlier, the "burden sharing" complaint is not valid. The United States gets enormous benefits from its Asian presence. But the realities of congressional and public opinion are such that it is important to convince Americans that its Asian allies are participating in the common defense.

Over the next several decades, there will probably be continued need for peacekeeping operations that serve U.S. and allied interests. The Balkans will require NATO–led peacekeepers for many years. Cyprus and the Middle East are other zones likely to consume peacekeeping resources for some time, as perhaps one day the Caucasus will if a peace settlement is reached over Nagorno-Karabakh. Regardless of all the modern technology available, peacekeeping is a labor-intensive business. Soldiers must be visible to reassure populations, arrest troublemakers, check that demarcation lines are respected, prevent confrontations, and perform other tasks as dictated by local circumstances. It also requires a large manpower base because units on peacekeeping duty are generally rotated into the region rather than permanently stationed there. The goal should be for Japan to contribute much more, perhaps as much as 5,000 troops at any time in such peacekeeping operations, including those in dangerous places. But again, this change will have to be gradual so as not to outpace its acceptance by the Japanese electorate and Japan's neighbors. Korea's contribution is likely to be more limited because the South Korean army is needed to defend the country, but the ROK could still increase its contribution (it has already participated in several PKO deployments, including East Timor). After unification, Korea could also contribute significant numbers of troops to peacekeeping activities (though given the cost of unification, its PKO activities may have to be underwritten by other states).

Such a development would enhance the image of Japan and Korea in the United States. It would show skeptics that these allies contribute to the common defense. For example, if there were a Japanese brigade in Bosnia it would greatly benefit Japan's image in the United States. It would also provide the SDF with useful experience on how to deploy and operate forces abroad.

Promoting the training and stationing of Japanese and Korean forces in the United States is another area that could be explored. Training in the United States offers the advantage of large spaces for military exercises that smaller countries with the population densities of Korea and Japan cannot provide their soldiers and airmen. This could also be an opportunity to proceed gradually with trilateral U.S.–ROK–Japanese training, perhaps a first time for peacekeeping operations, in the United States. Australia, which has a large unpopulated territory, could also participate in such schemes, hosting Japanese and Korean forces.

This could lead to the permanent establishment of ROK and Japanese army and air force bases in the United States. Joint training in the United States rather than in Asia could lessen the problem of social costs to Japanese and Koreans. Thus, part of the U.S.–Asian military interaction would be moved from the overcrowded Japanese and Korean countrysides to the empty deserts of the United States. This would also show Koreans and Japanese that the alliances are not a one-way street in which they alone host foreign soldiers, but a two-way alliance, with their own soldiers and airmen based permanently in the United States.

One of the problems of America's Northeast Asian policy has been a lack of coordination between U.S. policy toward Korea, Japan, China, and Taiwan. Northeast Asia is a strategic region, and American policy toward these four countries should flow from the same broad strategic concepts. The Guideline Review Process points to the traditional American policy of making Japan the anchor of America's strategy in Asia. Yet, the Clinton journey to China in 1998 gave the impression that Sino-American relations were paramount, and the desire to keep channels open to North Korea after the missile test raised questions about the U.S. commitment to Japan.

There are many reasons for America's problems in developing a coherent Northeast Asian policy. Its European policy has generally been integrated. America does not have separate "German policies," "Hungarian policies," or "Italian policies" because it has an itegrated European doctrine. But for a variety of historical and bureaucratic reasons it has seldom had a "Northeast Asia policy," and designing such a policy would be far more difficult.

First, America's regional allies, Japan, Korea, or Taiwan, are not integrated into anything resembling NATO and the European Union (and Taiwan does not even have official relations with the United States, Japan, or South Korea). Second, Japan and the ROK are allies and North Korea is a foe, but China is neither a friend nor an enemy, rendering policy-making more complex. Third, Asian countries are much more politically, economically, and culturally heterogeneous than European ones. Fourth, the U.S. military in Europe is under a single NATO umbrella, in which the army is clearly the dominant service; in Asia, the command arrangements for U.S. forces are more complex, with all four services heavily represented in the theater and the absence of a Korean-Japan alliance. Finally, bureaucratic and intellectual inertia would require a determined effort from the top to force all the elements in the civilian and military services to readjust their traditional arrangements and ways of thinking.

It would help U.S. policy if there were an integrated Northeast Asian perspective. This would require policy-makers to incorporate Japan, Korea, China, Taiwan, and the Russian Far East into a comprehensive vision of American policy in the region. It might also make it easier to control the often-unhealthy unilateral impulses of the United States in the field of trade. Trade sanctions against Asian exporters and other protectionist measures are particularly damaging to the interests of the United States in Asia (and, in turn, harm American consumers). If a stronger sense of "Northeast Asia" could be developed in the U.S. government, it might restrain some of these protectionist inclinations.

The United States and its allies cannot control the way in which North Korea will disappear, but it would help avoid problems if Washington, Tokyo, and Seoul jointly developed a framework for how the post-unification region should look. For example, it might make sense to address the issue of Korean denuclearization prior to unification. The United States might suggest a security guarantee to Korea, complete with U.S. forces, in exchange for Korea's promise not to acquire nuclear weapons, a move that would surely reassure Japan. It is also important for the United States to consider how China can be integrated into a post-settlement structure in a way that does not jeopardize allied interests but that also satisfies Korea's desire to avoid antagonizing its northern neighbor. Work toward developing multilateral organizations, something that is also of great interest to Koreans, should be among the efforts considered. But the most important task for the future is to ensure that U.S. forces remain in Korea and Japan after unification.

BIBLIOGRAPHY

Ahn Byong-Joon. "Korea–U.S. Alliance Toward Unification." *Korea Focus,* vol. 4:2, 1996.

Ahn Byong-Joon. "U.S. Forces in a Unified Korea." *Korea Focus,* vol. 5:3, 1997.

American Public Opinion & U.S. Foreign Policy 1999. Chicago, IL: Chicago Council on Foreign Relations. 12 February 1999. <http://www.ccfr.org/publications/opinion/opinion.html>.

Binnendijk, Hans, and Ronald N. Montaperto. *Strategic Trends in China.* Washington, D.C.: National Defense University, 1998.

Bogusky, Richard L. "The Impact of Korean Unification on Northeast Asia: American Security Challenges and Opportunities." *The Korea Journal of Defense Analysis,* vol. 10:1, 1998.

Chen Jian. *The China Challenge in the Twenty-First Century: Implications of U.S. Foreign Policy.* Washington, D.C.: United States Institute for Peace, June 1998.

Chen Jian. *China's Road to the Korean War.* New York, NY: Columbia University Press, 1994.

Cohen, William S. *The U.S. Security Strategy for the East-Asia Pacific.* Washington, D.C.: Department of Defense, Office of International Security Affairs, November 1998.

Craig, Albert M., John K. Fairbank, and Edwin O. Reischauer. *East Asia: Tradition and Transformation.* Boston, MA: Houghton Mifflin, 1989.

Crowley, James B. *Japan's Quest for Autonomy: National Security and Foreign Policy 1930–1938.* Princeton, NJ: Princeton University Press, 1966.

DeConde, Alexander. *A History of American Foreign Policy.* In *Global Power,* vol. 2, 3rd ed. New York, NY: Charles Scribners' Sons, 1978.

Defense Agency, Japan. *Defense of Japan.* Translated by The Japan Times, Ltd., 1998.

Dobson, William J. Review of "The Coming Conflict with China." *Survival,* vol. 34:3, 1997.

Dower, John W. *Empire and Aftermath: Yoshida Shigeru and the Japanese Experience, 1878–1954.* Cambridge, MA: Harvard University Press, 1988.

Dujarric, Robert. "The 'Emerging Markets' Mirage." *American Outlook*. Indianapolis, IN: Hudson Institute, Winter 1999.

Dujarric, Robert, ed. *Korea and Japan: Toward a New Partnership?* Indianapolis, IN: Hudson Institute, forthcoming.

Epstein, M., ed. *The Statesman's Yearbook: Statistical and Historical Annual of the States of the World for the Year 1928*. London: MacMillian and Co., 1928. 1929, 1937, 1930, 1933, and 1941 Yearbooks also used.

Feng Chen. "Rebuilding the Party's Normative Authority: China's Socialist Spiritual Civilization Campaign." *Problems of Post-Communism*, vol. 45:6, 1998.

Finer, S. E. *The History of Government,* vol. 2. London: Oxford University Press, 1997.

Finkelstein, David M. "China's Military Strategy." in James C. Mulvenon and Richard H. Yang, editors, *The People's Liberation Army in the Information Age*. Santa Monica, CA: RAND Corporation, 1999.

Fishburn, Dudley, ed. *The World in 1999*. The Economist Newspaper Limited, 1998.

Green, Michael J., editor. *Managing Change on the Korean Peninsula*, Independent Task Force Report. New York, NY: Council on Foreign Relations Press, 1998.

Grinker, Roy R. *Korea and Its Futures: Unification and the Unfinished War*. New York, NY: St. Martin's Press, 1998.

Han Yong-Sup. "Korea's Security Strategy for the 21st Century: Cooperation and Conflict." *Korea Focus,* vol. 5:4, 1997.

Horner, Charles. "Rising Sun, the Good Earth, and the U.S." *The National Interest*, Fall 1996.

Hosakawa Morihiro. "Are U.S. Troops in Japan Needed? Reforming the Alliance." *Foreign Affairs,* vol. 77:4, 1998.

Hosoya Chihiro. "Japan's Policies Toward Russia." In *Japan's Foreign Policy*, edited by J. W. Morley. New York: Columbia University Press, 1974.

Hunter, Brian, ed. *The Statesman's Yearbook: Statistical and Historical Annual of the States of the World for the Year 1997*. New York, NY: St. Martin's Press, 1997.

Information Office of the State Council of the People's Republic of China. *China's National Defense*. Beijing, July 1998.

International Institute for Strategic Studies. *The Military Balance 1997/98*. London: Oxford University Press, 1997.

Iriye, Akira. *The Cold War in Asia: A Historical Introduction*. Englewood Cliffs, NJ: Prentice Hall, 1974.

Iriye, Akira. *The Globalizing of America, 1913–1945*. In *The Cambridge History of American Foreign Relations*, vol. 3. New York, NY: Cambridge University Press, 1993.

Johnson, Chalmers. "The People Who Invented the Mechanical Nightingale." In *Showa: The Japan of Hirohito*, edited by C. Gluck and S. R. Graubard. New York: W.W. Norton & Co., 1992.

Johnston, Alastair I. "China's Militarized Interstate Dispute Behavior 1949–1992: A First Cut at the Data." *China Quarterly*, no. 153, March 1998.

Kang, C. S. Eliot. "Korean Unification: A Pandora's Box of Northeast Asia." *Asian Perspective*, vol. 20:2, 1996.

Kennedy, Paul. *The Rise and Fall of the Great Powers: Economic Change and Military Conflict from 1500 to 2000*. New York: Random House, 1989.

Kim Sung-Han. "The Future of the Korea–U.S. Alliance." *Korea and World Affairs*, Summer 1996.

Kim, T.W. "South Korea's: Nuclear Dilemmas," *Korea and World Affairs*. 16, Summer 1992.

Korean Ministry of Education. *Korean History for Ethnic Koreans Abroad*. Seoul: Korean Ministry of Education, 1998.

Kristol, Irving. "The Coming Clash of Welfare States." *American Outlook*, Hudson Institute, Winter 1999.

LaFeber, Walter. *The Clash: U.S. Japanese Relations Throughout History*. New York, NY: W.W. Norton, 1997.

Lee Dong-Bok. "Remembering and Forgetting: The Political Culture of Memory in Divided Korea." *Korea and World Affairs*, Fall 1995.

Levin, Norm. "Chapter 6." *Strategic Appraisal 1996*, edited by Z. Khalizad. Santa Monica, CA: RAND Corporation, 1996.

Lipset, Seymour M. *American Exceptionalism: A Double Edged Sword*. New York: W.W. Norton, 1996.

Lockwood, William W., *The Economic Development of Japan: Growth and Structural Change 1868–1938*. Princeton, NJ: Princeton University Press, 1954.

Mochizuki, Mike M. *Japan: Domestic Change and Foreign Policy*. Santa Monica, CA: RAND Corporation, 1995.

Mochizuki, Mike M. "A New Bargain for a Stronger Alliance." In *Toward a True Alliance: Restructuring U.S. –Japan Security Relations*, edited by M. M. Mochizuki. Washington, D.C.: Brookings Institution Press, 1997.

Montaperto, Ronald N. *Strategic Assessment 1988*. Edited by H. Binnendijk. Washington, D.C.: National Defense University, 1998.

Nack Young An. "Korea in the East Asian Dynamic." *Korea and World Affairs*, Spring 1995.

Niksch, Larry. "North Korea's Coming ICBM." *Nautilus Institute*. 10 February 1999 <http://www.nautilus.org/napsnet/for a/ 9903A_Niksch.html>.

Nish, Ian. "Japan's Policies Toward Britain." In *Japan's Foreign Policy*, edited by J. W. Morley. New York: Columbia University Press, 1974.

O'Hanlon, Michael. "Can High Technology Bring U.S. Troops Home?" *Foreign Policy*, no. 113, Winter 1998–99.

O'Hanlon, Michael. "Restructuring U.S. Forces and Bases in Japan." In *Toward a True Alliance*, edited by M. Mochizuki. Washington, D.C.: Brookings Institution Press, 1997.

Odell, Robert, editor. *China, the United States, and Japan: Implications for Future U.S. Security Strategy in Asia*, 1997 Annual Conference Summary, Center for Naval Analyses.

Odom, William E. *The Collapse of the Soviet Military*. New Haven, CT: Yale University Press, 1998.

Odom, William E. "Transforming the Military." *Foreign Affairs*, vol. 76:4, 1997.

Office of International Security Affairs. *United States Security Strategy for the East Asia–Pacific Region*. Washington, D.C.: Department of Defense, February 1995.

Olson, Mancur, and Richard Zeckhauser. "An Economic Theory of Alliances." *Review of Economics and Statistics*, vol. 48:3, 1966.

Overholt, William H. "Korea: To the Market via Socialism." *Emerging Markets Research: Asia*. Singapore: BankBoston, 21 July 1998.

Packard, George R., III. *Protest in Tokyo: The Security Treaty Crisis of 1960*. Princeton, NJ: Princeton University Press, 1966.

Paxton, John, ed. *The Statesman's Yearbook: Statistical and Historical Annual of the States of the World for the Year 1990*. New York, NY: St. Martin's Press, 1990.

Scales, Robert, and Paul Van Riper. "Preparing for War in the 21st Century." *Strategic Review*, vol. 25:3, 1997.

Steel, Ronald. "The Hard Questions: Re-Orient." *The New Republic*, 8 & 15 September 1997.

Stuart, Douglas T., and William T. Tow. *A U.S. Strategy for Asia-Pacific: Building a Multipolar Balance of Power System in Asia*. Oxford: Oxford University Press, 1996.

Stueck, William. *The Korean War: An International History*. Princeton, NJ: Princeton University Press, 1995.

Tamamoto Masaru. "The Ideology of Nothingness." *World Policy Journal*, Spring 1994.

Turner, Barry. *The Statesman's Year Book 1998–1999: The Essential Political and Economic Guide to All the Countries in the World*. New York: St. Martin's Press, 1998.

"View from the Summit." *The Economist*, 27 March 1999.

Vogel, Ezra F., ed. *Living with China: U.S.–China Relations in the Twenty-First Century*. New York, NY: W.W. Norton & Co., 1997.

Warner, V. J. "Technology Favors Future Land Forces." *Strategic Review*, vol. 26:3, 1998.

Weathersby, Kathryn. "New Russian Documents on the Korean War." *The Cold War in Asia*, Woodrow Wilson International Center for Scholars, Cold War International History Project Bulletin, no. 6–7.

Zhang Shu Guang. *Mao's Military Romanticism: China and the Korean War, 1950–1953*. Lawrence, KS: University Press of Kansas, 1995.

Zoelick, Robert B. "China: What Engagement Should Mean." *National Interest*, no. 46, Winter 1996–7.

DATE DUE

HIGHSMITH #45230

Printed
in USA